A Special Gift . . .

To: ______________________________

From: ______________________________

Message: ______________________________

____

____

____

____

____

MAKE GOD YOUR CEO!

10 STEPS TO AN ABUNDANTLY BLESSED BUSINESS

Terri Rhem Robinson

iUniverse, Inc.
Bloomington

Make God Your CEO!
10 Steps to an Abundantly Blessed Business

iUniverse books may be ordered through booksellers or by contacting:

iUniverse
1663 Liberty Drive
Bloomington, IN 47403
www.iuniverse.com
1-800-Authors (1-800-288-4677)

ISBN: 978-1-4759-0784-1 (sc)
ISBN: 978-1-4759-0785-8 (ebk)

Printed in the United States of America

iUniverse rev. date: 04/26/2012

Contents

Dedication

I dedicate this book to the glory and honor of my spiritual Life Coach, Lord and Personal Savior, ***Jesus Christ.*** *Through Him* and the power of the Holy Spirit, I pray that this body of work will bring ultimate glory to GOD—my blessed Heavenly Father, Creator and *CEO of my life!*

"That I may publish with the voice of thanksgiving, and tell of all thy wondrous works."
Psalm 26:7

Acknowledgements

Thank you GOD! Through your *amazing grace*, mercy and guidance, I have finally completed one of the most meaningful works of my life! I have spent the last 15+ years—*writing, editing, revising, reviewing* and *DOING* my best to *live* the 10 steps outlined in ***"Make God Your CEO"***.

In this time of economic uncertainty, high unemployment and increasing workplace woes, this book is needed *NOW* more than ever! God, my spiritual CEO, has made it IMPOSSIBLE for me NOT to share my personal testimonies with the world! *To God, I give ALL the glory!*

I could not have completed this body of work without the awesome support of my loving family, loyal friends, business associates and career acquaintances. Thanks for providing me with the insights, inspirations, life lessons and support for the creation of ***Make God Your CEO! 10 Steps to Abundant Blessings in Business!*** *I pray that EVERY reader will positively benefit from the spiritual principles mentioned throughout this book. Prepare to be blessed . . .*

"For the Lord God is a sun and shield; the Lord will give grace and mercy; no good thing will he withhold from them that *walk* uprightly." Psalms 84:11

Introduction

"SURRENDERING Total Control of My Career to GOD!"

__CEO__—aka, ***Chief Executive Officer;***
The highest ranking executive in a company whose main responsibilities include developing and implementing high-level strategies, making major corporate decisions, managing the overall operations and resources of a company, and acting as the main point of communication between the board of directors and the corporate operations.
(Investopedia Online Dictionary)

Is your current career bordering on *'bankruptcy'*—void of the *passion, purpose* or *prosperity* you desire? Is your current job on life-support, possibly one management decision away from elimination? Are you currently one of the millions of Americans facing unemployment through no fault of your own—victims of a brutal, unrelenting economy or poor leadership decisions? Have you been thinking that no one's listening or cares about your workplace woes or personal plights? If you answered 'YES' to any of these questions, then, ***'Make God Your CEO'*** was written with *YOU in mind!*

Once upon a time, not too terribly long ago—I was on a dead-end career path, facing involuntary unemployment for the *first time* in my career. The uncertainty of how I would help support the basic needs of my family of five kept me up many nights and awakened me before dawn several mornings. Then, GOD gave me *THE PLAN* to resurrect my career and to help me achieve my life's dreams*!*

I was inspired to write, *"Make God Your CEO!"* in a most peculiar way. While driving down a Georgia highway one rainy afternoon, I found myself deep in thought, contemplating my next career move. Suddenly, I spoke the words, *"If you want to succeed in business, make God your CEO!"* It seemed I had no thoughts of this statement prior to that very moment.

Immediately, I turned off my radio and began to openly converse with God. I knew a directive that powerful could only have come from Him. He directed me to recall my most trying and triumphant experiences throughout my career. I remembered how He had coached me through so many difficult challenges on the job. I also recalled how He had shown me favor in so many other work-related situations. I became encouraged when I thought about how loyal and good God had been to me throughout my entire career. His message to each of us is simple, ***"He (God) 'alone' is in ultimate control of our careers. He is an out-of-this-world, compassionate, proven leader who is more than capable of successfully guiding us through ANY challenges we may face on or off our respective jobs!"***

I've discovered throughout my career that every time I've put my TOTAL FAITH in God to direct the outcome of my efforts, I have achieved tremendous success, joy and personal fulfillment. Early in my career, I began *consciously* appointing God as my spiritual CEO through my loving, loyal Life Coach Jesus Christ. God's ultimate employee handbook—***The Holy Bible***—has served as a fail-proof guide for my personal and business endeavors for as long as I can remember.

After being burned a few times via the self-serving politics of workplace peers, I knew that I could not leave the fate of my career exclusively in the hands of *man nor woman!* National and local news stories reveal the greed-oriented tactics of CEOs from Wall Street to the suspicious business practices of companies near *your street.* I have turned to God to help me get through many challenging career trials and tribulations. I've depended upon Him to protect me from the personal attacks of unscrupulous, self-serving peers. God has a protection plan that's out of this world! There isn't a corporate executive on earth that can match His credentials, exceed His accomplishments, master His management style or beat His benefits package.

Let's go back for a moment to the day God gave me the awesome assignment to write, *"Make God Your CEO!"* I was at a major crossroads in my own career. The security of my job of 8+ years as a Marketing Manager with a Fortune 100 telecommunications company had just been eliminated. Although I had been given the option of relocation to the state of Dallas, Texas—with my job intact, my husband and I opted to remain in Georgia for personal reasons. We had made our home together in Atlanta since just before our marriage in August 1986. Our desire was to ensure our kids grew up close to our family members located in Florida, North Carolina and Mississippi. As a result of our decision to remain in Atlanta, *on January 1, 1996*, I found myself unemployed, unsure of my future and contemplating what to do once my dwindling severance payments ended in a few short months. This was the first *involuntary* termination I had experienced since the beginning of my professional career. Prior to that time, the only jobs that had ended abruptly for me were those I had voluntarily left behind for promotions to positions of greater responsibilities and increased financial compensation.

For the first time in my life, I became a ranking member of the 'unemployed'. This new-found freedom and unstructured time alone proved exciting, exhilarating and tad bit *frightening!* I was temporarily relieved to be free from the stresses and constraints of Corporate America to pursue my creative endeavors. However, I was also a little nervous and apprehensive about the prospect of not having a regular bi-weekly income flowing into my household for much longer.

Our household had always operated on a double-income spending plan. Although he hadn't said it, I knew my husband was a little nervous about the prospect of solely carrying the load of the household expenses for an indefinite period of time. I knew I would have to find another means of income before my severance payments ended. My strong faith and belief in God and my recollection of the many times He had helped me to overcome many trials and tribulations—was a source of comfort to me. I knew He would help my family through our 'wilderness experience'. I just didn't know *HOW* or *WHEN!*

Two weeks prior to the receipt of my last severance check, ***God,*** my *awesome* CEO, blessed my family in a big way! I know it was GOD who influenced my former employer to hire me back in a newly created *Marketing Communications Manager* position based in *Atlanta, Georgia!* I knew God was the primary force behind this new opportunity, because the position required someone with my exact job experiences and creative background! This new position was also two job grades *higher* than my previous position which included a significantly higher salary. So, after 3 months away on severance pay, I went back to work at the same company with a promotion, a five-figure salary increase, excellent health and retirement benefits and a refreshing, enthusiastic new *attitude of gratitude!* In addition, my previous employment with the company was bridged as "continued service" and I received an additional three and a half weeks of *paid* vacation to take at my leisure later that year!

God not only provided for my family's basic needs, he had also given me a wonderful new opportunity to make a substantial income doing the kind of work I *loved*. ***God is truly the BEST in the BLESSING business!*** I share this testimony to let you know that what He did for me, God can do for YOU too! He is ready and willing to turn your employment situation around and set your career on a higher, more secure ground!

Although God had blessed me with the opportunity to do the kind of work I loved, I continued to contemplate the powerful directive he had given me that rainy Georgia day. I thought about the incredible career challenges I had overcome including unforeseen setbacks and the blessings of so many successes. Each experience serves as positive confirmations of God's powerful love, grace and incredible mercy in my life.

I am honored to pay tribute to God's awesome influence throughout my career by sharing some of my most inspiring personal testimonies throughout the pages of this book. It is my intent to use my life and my love for the Lord to provide proven steps to help get your career back on track and moving BOLDLY toward your dreams and goals. I hope you will draw strength and encouragement for whatever you're facing and apply the unique spiritual principles enclosed to advance your professional and personal life to new heights!

By the world's standards, the salary for an outstanding leader such as God with an unmatched record for success would be far greater than today's corporate giants could afford. I imagine if I were a recruiter or head-hunter attempting to sell a corporation on God's abilities, I would confidently and enthusiastically say:

"GOD is responsible for more business successes than any CEO in history. He has done many marvelous works throughout His career—far too many to list. However, you may get a peek at some of His most spectacular works chronicled in the all-time, best-selling book, 'The Holy Bible.' To view His best work—just look in the mirror! His trademark is 'LIFE' itself. God has never been late to work, missed a deadline or taken a day off. He truly leads by example. God is in the ultimate business of CREATING, BLESSING, PROTECTING and SAVING LIVES. God thinks of each of His employees as His children. He finds joy in leading everyone under His employment to rich, rewarding, prosperous careers and blessed, fulfilling lives. He encourages all who follow Him to make Jesus Christ—His incredibly talented son and very capable right-hand man—their daily Life Coach, Lord and Personal Savior. In addition, God encourages His team of followers to, 'don't leave home without the Holy Spirit.' God, Jesus Christ and the Holy Spirit comprise the ultimate leadership dream team.

God has an incredible knack for building multi-billion dollar empires on a whim. Nothing is too difficult for this CEO. The bigger the challenge, the more He enjoys showing off His incredible

'problem-solving abilities'. Unlike many of today's busy CEOs of the world, God is extremely approachable. He encourages every employee, from the mailroom clerk and custodial staff to the Chief Operations Office and Company President, to call Him ANYTIME with whatever their concerns may be throughout the day or night. You'll never find His phone forwarded to voicemail or His schedule over-booked. He's always close by—ready, willing and able to lead His team of followers to VICTORY!

God is a loving, forgiving, inspiring, one-of-a-kind leader. His name alone commands respect, praise and adoration from people all over the world. Even the most cynical business analysts or devout atheist have to respect God's unparalleled feats in business. There is little, if anything one can criticize regarding God's impeccable list of credentials, countless corporate successes and His extensive humanitarian efforts.

I could go on and on about this amazing CEO candidate, but it would probably be best if you met Him yourself. He's available to begin working for you at anytime. All you have to do is seek Him . . .

THE PURPOSE OF THIS BOOK:

"Make God Your CEO" will arm you with a proven step-by-step game plan for recharging your career and living a more fulfilling, joyous professional and personal life!

My hope is that you will gain strength and comfort through the applications of the powerful biblical scriptures contained in this book. Each scripture beautifully illustrates and supports each spiritual step to success.

I pray you are motivated through the sharing of real-life personal testimonies, inspiring poems and empowering affirmations.

I encourage you to allow the ongoing presence of God in your life to lead you *up* a career path filled with unlimited *possibilities!*

SUGGESTION: *Record the affirmations at the end of each chapter on note cards. Keep them with you at all times and recite them daily.*

"They think the chief executive is all powerful, but the only thing that is all powerful is GOD!"

The Late Roberto C. Goizueta
Former CEO,
The Coca-Cola Company
Atlanta, GA

Step #1

SEEK God's Guidance at the Start of Each Day

"Evening and morning and at noon, will I pray, and cry aloud: And He shall hear my voice."
Psalm 55:17 (KJV)

"A Daily Dose of Vitamin G"

I can recall a time in my life, not too terribly long ago, when I would awaken each morning just before the alarm sounded. I would then drag myself out of bed and shuffle up the hall to my in-home office with a pretty lengthy mental list of all the tasks I hoped to accomplish for the day.

Once closed away inside my private sanctuary, I'd become united with my day planner and attempt to prioritize obligations, errands and pending business appointments for the day. This exercise required a great deal of concentration as I tried to match the hours available in the day with the demands of a full-time corporate job, the responsibilities of running a small, growing business as well as the inherit duties of being a wife, mom and household maintenance manager. My goal was to complete my daily planning ritual before my precious, yet demanding, three year son awakened for the morning.

I would often become overwhelmed at the 'things-to-do' list I prepared and wonder, *"God, how in the world am I ever going to accomplish all these things?"* But, before I would allow God to answer me, I would start packing up everything I felt I needed to take into my corporate job for the day. I would then rush downstairs to prepare breakfast for my family. Inevitably, soon after starting breakfast, I would hear the footsteps of my young son descending the stairs and his sleepy, high-pitched voice calling out, *"Mommy, where are you?"* As he'd round the corner to see me standing at the stove, he'd smile, run to me with hands held high and plant the biggest, sloppiest kiss ever on my face! After our mutual exchange of, "I love you", my morning would be primarily devoted to him from that point on.

After ensuring he'd eaten most of his breakfast, I'd dress my son for school and encourage him to read or watch one of his favorite children's television programs while I got ready for work. I would then drive him to school (if his father wasn't available to do so) and attempt to find the quickest route to work around rush hour traffic and time-consuming stop-and-go school bus routes.

As a result of carrying out this rigorous morning routine day in, day out over an extended period of time, I began to feel anxious, overwhelmed, frustrated and depleted of energy by the time I finally arrived to the demands of my corporate job each morning. I remember asking myself questions like, *"Are my anxieties and frustrations normal? I wonder how others handle the demands of being working parents with high-pressure corporate jobs. Am I going to be able to keep up this routine for very much longer? Should I start exercising more to increase my energy? But when would I have time? Perhaps I should consider taking vitamins—but what kind?"*

One particular morning, I was sitting at my desk at work, staring at my extensive things-to-do list, starting to feel a bit overwhelmed when the telephone rang. My friend, Diane, called to convey her usual perky "good morning!" It was great to hear her calming, enthusiastic voice on the other end of the line. She knew me well enough to tell by my greeting and the tone of my voice that something was terribly wrong.

After asking how I was doing, I'm sure Diane thought she had opened the lid to Pandora's Box. I began venting all my built up frustrations *nonstop* for the next several minutes. I explained how overwhelmed I felt by the demands of my job, the responsibilities of being a relatively new mother, my desires to be a more supportive wife while managing every facet of running my household. My friend listened patiently as I continued to verbalize my frustrations.

As I took a brief moment to catch my breath, Diane quickly interjected her cure for eliminating anxieties at the start of each day. My dear friend recommended a daily dose of **Vitamin G**. ***'G'*** is for ***GOD***! She shared her daily ritual of starting each day in prayer, supplication and praise to God. She said it was the most important, peaceful part of her day.

The following is my friend Diane's prescription for **a daily dose of Vitamin 'G':**

1. ***Awaken at least 30-60 minutes earlier each morning*** before your family awakens to spend time alone with God *Don't forget to set you alarm the night before!*

2. ***Find a quiet, private place for quite meditation on biblical scriptures*** in or near your home.

3. ***Pray to God*** about the biblical passages you read and seek discernment on their application to *your* life.

4. ***Appeal to God*** to solve any challenges/concerns you may be facing in your professional or personal life. He is *THE ULTIMATE EXPERT* on ANY trials and tribulations we may face.

5. ***Seek God's guidance*** to accomplish those tasks He deems are most important to His divine mission for you.

Since Diane's day was planned and ordered by God, she could boldly, confidently face each day with assurance that the outcome of her day would be successful. I thought, *"Wow! What a refreshing way to start the day!"* Although I had thought of God often throughout the day, I hadn't routinely practiced spending time alone in meditation with Him *every* morning. I told my friend that I was willing to try her spiritual cure for anxiety in an effort to bring more peace, balance and order back into my life. She offered to assist me by calling me over the next several mornings to pray together and to share and discuss powerful, affirming biblical scriptures. We practiced this inspiring new ritual for the next few weeks until it became *my* daily routine.

I soon found that my daily dose of Vitamin 'G' was just the cure I needed to eliminate anxiety and get control of my life again. I don't worry anymore about what I don't accomplish during the day. I tend to get the most important things done first—spending time with God, spending time with my family, attending to their needs and addressing as many business concerns as time and priorities allow. Any tasks I can't accomplish today, I pray God will give me another opportunity to complete them on another day.

Each of us can alter our morning routines just a little to allow more time alone with God. He wants more of our time each weekday (not just during church services on the weekends). He desires to arm us with the confidence, peace of mind and capacity to do *His will* in the world.

The following poem beautifully illustrates the importance of putting God *first* at the start of each day. Read it, apply it and be encouraged . . .

The Difference

(Author Unknown)

***I got up early one morning
and rushed right into the day;
I had so much to accomplish, that I
didn't have time to pray.***

***Problems just tumbled about me;
and heavier came each task.
"Why doesn't God help me?" I
wondered. He answered, "You didn't ask."***

***I wanted to see joy and beauty,
but the day toiled on, gray and bleak;
I wondered, "Why God didn't show me?"
He said, "But you didn't seek."***

***I tried to come into God's presence;
I used all my keys at the lock.
God gently and lovingly chided,
"My child, you didn't knock."***

***I woke up early this morning,
and paused before entering
the day; I had so much to
accomplish that I had to
take time to pray.***

Summary:

Our inherit responsibilities as spouses, parents, sisters, brothers, aunts, uncles, grandparents, co-workers, managers, business owners and members of a diverse, fast-paced society are filled with tremendous pressures and anxieties. God is the key source for guidance and peace in the midst of life's trials and storms. He is *ALWAYS* available to meet those who seek Him. Trust His loving mercy, favor and grace to help you live a more victorious life through Jesus Christ!

Exercise:

1. *Do you routinely set aside time to pray to God and plan for each day?*

2. *If YES, describe your normal routine to prepare for your day.*

3. *If NO, set a date to begin this worthwhile morning ritual and commit to do it for 30 consecutive days.*

4. *How can you alter your current morning routine to schedule more 'quality one-on-one time' with God?*

5. *Share your new praying and planning ritual with at least 3 other people.*

6. *Ask at least one trusted Christian friend to pray with you for 21 consecutive mornings.*

Affirmation:

"Seeking God's guidance is the first priority of my day. Honoring Him in all I do is my ultimate goal in life!"

Step #2

CREATE Joy on Your Job Using Your God-Given Gifts

"Neglect not the gift that is in thee . . ."
1 Timothy 4:14 (KJV)

"And whatsoever ye do, do it heartily, as to the Lord, and not unto men; Knowing that of the Lord ye shall receive the reward of the inheritance; For ye serve the Lord Christ."
Colossians 3:23-24 (KJV)

"Creating Opportunity"

Shortly after my wedding in August 1986, I decided to resign from my position as a flight attendant with a major US airline. I had been based in Detroit Michigan throughout my engagement and decided to find a job based in Atlanta, Georgia so I could be closer to my new husband.

I accepted a position as an assistant store manager at a chic, trendy women's boutique located in a mall in an Atlanta suburb. Besides the obvious perks of working around beautiful designer clothes and gorgeous fashion accessories all day, I also met and assisted interesting shoppers from all walks of life. I was also second in charge of store operations behind my store manager, Patti. I spent at least 60% of my time helping my boss run the store, motivate, train and recruit new members of our sales team. The remainder of my time was spent actually *selling* to help my store reach its sales goals.

One of the store manager's daily responsibilities was to review the store's sales plan. She would determine each associate's sales goals based upon the hours an individual was scheduled to work that day. She would place this information in a sales plan book near the cash register and expected each associate to review her sales goals shortly after reporting to work each day.

Because little time was spent by our leadership team strategizing *how* and *what* we would do to achieve sales plan, our store was often unsuccessful in reaching our revenue goals. Missing sales goals week after week eventually took its toll on many of our associates who were either fired for poor performances or eventually quit from the pressures of struggling to meet their quotas. Inevitably, we were *always* recruiting for qualified sales help.

One day, Patti suggested that I take over the sales planning process for our store. Specifically, she asked me to track each associate's sales efforts on a weekly basis. Then, compare their results with the weekly sales plan to determine how close we were to achieving our sales objectives. I happily stepped up to the challenge. After observing her hastily set sales objectives each day and witnessing her anger when objectives went unmet, I had several ideas on how to make this process more positive, productive and fun for everyone! I also hoped to decrease constant turnover on our sales team.

Our management staff consisted of a store manager (Patti), first assistant store manager (me) and a second assistant store manager named *Lynn*. Up until that point, the three of us had spent very little time discussing our store's sales objectives or devising plans to achieve them. As a result, we couldn't possibly appear as a cohesive, focused, unified management team to our sales associates.

I decided to address our communications deficiencies by using my God-given gift of creativity to write and illustrate a '*how-to*' booklet entitled, *"Guidelines for Management Cohesiveness"*. In the booklet, I suggested strategies for improving communication between members of our management team as well as tips for training, motivating and inspiring our sales team to reach their individual sales goals. I illustrated the book with cartoon characters which actually resembled members of our in-store management team.

I hoped that my peers would welcome the ideas in my booklet and utilize my suggestions to make positive changes in our store. I scheduled a time to present my ideas to my management peers just before our store opened for business one morning. My peers not only appreciated my creative efforts, they *welcomed* ALL my suggestions! The store manager was quite honored that I featured a likeness of her throughout the pages of my booklet. She ensured that a copy of the guidelines was quickly sent to our District and Regional Managers. Our Regional Manager was so impressed with my work she sent a copy to our Vice-President of Store Operations in New York City. Our corporate VP of Store Operations, in turn, sent copies of my booklet to management teams in over **300** stores throughout the country! Shortly thereafter, I received a complementary memo from the corporate office recognizing my initiative and extra efforts on behalf of store sales teams throughout our company.

My management's appreciation for my ideas fueled my desires to do even more to contribute to our company's success. Next, I suggested themes for sales contests we could implement to increase revenues and motivate our sales teams. Again, our management team welcomed my suggestions and provided additional input and ideas for seasonal sales contests. I was happy to create colorful posters, motivational signs and sales plan sheets for each contest. I placed inspirational messages next to the time clock, in the employee lounge and next to the cash register for our team to view throughout the day. We began projecting sales objectives at least one month in advance and enlisting the input of members of our sales team to devise strategies for achieving them. We encouraged our sales associates to call their customers to inform them when exciting new merchandise arrived. In addition, we encouraged then to ask for referrals from satisfied, repeat clients. As a result of implementing our new, aggressive game plan, our associates began to meet and *exceed* their sales objectives on a frequent basis. Our store gradually began achieving our weekly sales plans. We eventually became recognized as one of the highest sales volume stores in our district!

I found joy in my job using my God-given gifts to improve communication and cohesiveness within our company. I started where I was, used what I had and did what I could to positively impact the people around me. In addition to the thanks I received from my team members and upper management, I received a big promotion just a few months later. My new assignment was Assistant to the Regional Director—supporting and inspiring the success of at least 25 stores throughout the Southeast!

I created the following poem, *"Pennies on the Pavement"* to inspire you to reach beyond any self-imposed limitations to achieve your unique goals in life. I believe that opportunities exist *all around us* for God to use us to make a positive difference in the world. Have you stopped to embrace *your,* 'pennies (opportunities) on the pavement' (of life)?

Pennies on the Pavement

By Terri Rhem Robinson

Today,

I found a penny on the pavement—
glistening, shining, sparkling and new.

I almost passed over it in my hurried pace;
I nearly missed its distinct hue.

You see, 'pennies on the pavement'
are symbolic of 'life' and 'opportunities'
scattered about us each day;

To create a new product, to deliver a
great service, and to attract good customers
who pay!

So, let the next time you see a penny
on the pavement, be a remember of what it
truly means;

Stop! Kneel Down! Pick it up!
Embrace it!

And, TRUST IN GOD to help you
realize your dreams!

Summary:

We each have spiritual gifts we can use to produce positive results in our lives and the lives of others. Through our relationship with God, *unlimited abilities* and *possibilities* reside in and around each of us. When we apply God-given gifts to contribute to the greater good of the people and organizations we serve, we can achieve amazing results that can positively impact our respective jobs and our world!

Exercise:

1. *What are some of the challenges you're facing in your current job situation?*

2. *What talents, experiences, skills, can you use to help solve some of your current career challenges?*

3. *What action(s) will you take TODAY to begin solving the challenges you are facing in your workplace or home life?*

Affirmation:

"I increase my success in life when I use my God-given gifts to achieve my goals, to positively contribute to the success of those around me and to ultimately bring glory and honor to GOD!"

Step #3

APPLY Prayer, Planning and Patience to Open Doors to Unlimited Opportunities

"Be anxious for nothing; But in everything by prayer and supplication with thanksgiving let your requests be made known to God. And the peace of God which surpasses all comprehension shall guide your hearts and your minds in Christ Jesus."
Philippians 4:6 (NIV)

"Name It and Claim It"

My tenure as a former Corporate Events Manager for a Fortune 500 telecommunications company was one of the most rewarding positions I held earlier in my career. Earning this opportunity had been no easy feat. As many as 39 qualified candidates throughout the company had applied for the same position I was seeking. The job as *Events Manager* was viewed by company employees as a *glamorous, high-profile, marketing position* filled with lots of perks. This position was one of only two that existed in an internationally renowned company of over 15,000 employees.

When the position was initially advertised on the company's employment bulletin board, I was working as an Administrative Coordinator in the Telemarketing Sales Department. One day, while delivering copies of the latest sales reports to our Sales Director, his secretary—who happened to be a dear friend of mine—mentioned that she saw an OPEN Events Manager position posted on our employee bulletin board. She thought the job suited my outgoing personality and printed a copy of the listing for me to review. The position was with the staff of our company's Atlanta-based Applied Technology Center (aka, ATC). The listing included the qualifications for the job, salary range, name and phone number of the assigned Human Resources recruiter. The ATC served as the showplace for Fortune 500 & Fortune 100 client prospects to visit with our company. Ultimately, current and potential clients would view presentations and demonstrations during their visits in an effort to determine if they would like to award our company lucrative contracts for their telecommunications needs.

What my dear friend didn't realize, I had often *dreamed* of being a successful Events Manager for our company! It's not like I wanted the current Events Manager to lose her job, I just thought that particular position was simply perfect for *me*! I often observed and admired how the chic, leggy, red-headed, blue-eyed bombshell named *Donna* had performed as the current Events Manager. She exuded a perky, yet authoritative persona in the presence of our visiting guests. Her keen sense of humor and quick wit kept our clients chuckling as she met their limousines in our massive, marble lobby or on elevator rides during their tours of our building. She seemed to truly enjoy taking great care of our customers from the moment she met them in the main lobby to the time she said good-bye to them at the end of their visits with us.

I knew that my experience as a former flight attendant for a major airline had helped me prepare for this new career opportunity of serving traveling business professionals. I was excited to have the opportunity to apply for such a great job. I immediately thanked God aloud for this opportunity and verbally *claimed it as MINE!* I had faith that if I made my desires known to God and firmly believed I was worthy of this wonderful new job, I had a great chance of getting it! And with that, I picked up the closest telephone and called the Human Resources contact named on the employment listing to schedule an informational interview.

I submitted my resume and application the very next day. Shortly thereafter, I was scheduled for a series of interviews with the hiring department's staff. Because the Applied Technology Center was off limits to most company employees, I had several questions about what actually happened behind the unusually thick double glass doors on the Parking 3 level of our building. The staff appeared to appreciate my intrigue and the questions I had prepared for them.

Upon successfully answering a battery of interview questions with the ATC staff, my last and most critical interview was granted with the ATC Director. In hindsight, that interview was one of the most intense interview sessions I've had in my life! I must admit, I was a little nervous when the Human Resources recruiter called me prior to my interview with the ATC Director to inform me that the field of candidates had been narrowed down from 39 to only 2—me and another "undisclosed" candidate. To top it off, members of the center staff had warned me that the ATC Director had a reputation for chewing up and spitting out anyone who didn't meet his expectations. In addition, I had heard that he was *extremely* satisfied with the performance of the previous Events Manager who had recently been promoted to another position within his department. So, ultimately, I would be competing with the track record of the former Events Manager and the qualifications of the mystery candidate.

The day of my final interview with the ATC Director, I spent the beginning of the day praying to God. I asked Him to remove any fear or anxiety that might creep into my subconscious and potentially sabotage my efforts to have a great interview. By the time I reported to the ATC Director's office, I was feeling quite confident and optimistic about my impending interview. I knew I had what it took to be the company's next Events Manager. I arrived about 10-15 minutes early for my interview.The Director's secretary invited me to have a seat for a few moments while she announced my arrival to her boss. A few moments later, a rather distinguished looking gentleman with salt-n-pepper hair, a thick mustache and closely-shaven beard appeared in the doorway. We quickly made our introductions, shook hands and he invited me to join him in his office for, what he termed, *a little talk.* Once seated at a small, round mahogany conference table in his office, the Director quickly began asking a series of questions he had extracted from information presented on my resume. I noticed a copy of my resume lying in an open folder on the table in front of him. I also noticed that he had highlighted a number of areas throughout my resume with red ink. There were also several notations scribbled down the page in the margins on either side.

I found the Director's questions to be quite probing and blunt. Initially, I felt I was doing a pretty good job of answering every question he hurled my way. That is, until he asked one question regarding my past employment history that caught me totally off guard. After adding up the total time I had spent in jobs since college and dividing that number by the five different jobs I'd held, Mr. Macatee inferred that I probably wouldn't stick around for long if given the opportunity to serve as his department's next Events Manager.

I was determined to prove the Director wrong! I had made up my mind that ***I*** was going to be his company's next Events Manager and there wasn't a thing he could say that was going to deter me from reaching my goal.Although his comments predicting my potentially short tenure with his department surprised me, I managed to maintain my composure. I quietly called on God for a counter response to his comments. After, what appeared a lengthy silence on my part, I confidently gave my rebuttal. I asked for just a moment to review the order of my employment history and to explain what unique circumstances prompted me to change jobs so frequently over the past 3+ years. The Director granted the time I needed to explain my patchy work history.

I methodically moved down my resume explaining each position I'd held and what qualities and skills I mastered in each position that made me the best candidate to serve as his next Events Manager. Then, I explained that each change in past employment was actually to positions of greater responsibility and/or compensation. I assured him that I was looking forward to the demands of the Events Manager position and welcomed the opportunity to become a contributing member of his ATC team. I stated that I would be dedicated to making a positive contribution to his department's objectives and to the overall success of the company for as long as I'm needed. I could tell that he sincerely appreciated my candor and honesty in answering his questions. I think that any initial reservations he had about hiring me were quickly put to rest after our conversation. I left the final outcome of my interview in God's hands—my high capable CEO. Mr. Macatee decided to take the upcoming Thanksgiving holiday weekend to mull over his decision of *WHO* would be his next Events Manager. I walked away from his office that day feeling strangely confident that the job was already *mine!*

My suspicions were confirmed by the Tuesday following the long Thanksgiving weekend. I received a phone call from Human Resources early that morning informing me that the ATC Director wanted to make a verbal offer to *me* for the Events Manager position. *I was ecstatic!* Of course, I accepted the job *immediately.* I thanked God aloud right then and there as I prepared to become a successful, contributing member of the ATC presentation team.

In my first year as an Events Manager, I was determined to make a positive impact in my new department. I took on projects no one else really wanted and volunteered for challenging projects that few wanted to do. In addition, I mastered the responsibilities of the Events Manager position. I took joy in "spoiling" our visiting customers by ensuring their time with our company was positive and productive. My efforts didn't go unnoticed. The ATC Director rewarded my enthusiasm and dedication to the success of his department with a ***1*** (one)—***EXCELLENT*** rating on my annual performance review. He informed me that a "1" rating is rarely given throughout the company. However, he felt that I had truly earned this high honor through my dedication and positive contributions to the overall success of his department throughout the previous year. I was both humbled and honored by my Director's confidence in my abilities. I was promoted to Senior Events Manager shortly thereafter. My new responsibilities included traveling throughout the country to recruit and train new Events Managers to support and staff new Applied Technology Centers in other key cities.

Had I dismissed or overlooked the listing for the Events Manager position, I would have missed out of the career opportunity of a lifetime! Instead, I pursued the position with confidence and conviction and *won*!

Summary:

Unique opportunities come our way each day. We must be prepared to grasp and act on them *immediately* to achieve our dreams. Our future successes and happiness is dependent upon the plans and actions we take today. Seek God's guidance to determine the positive direction you would like your life to progress and ***GO FOR IT***!

Exercise:

1. *Have you decided what your next career move will be? What is it (provide a detailed description)?*

2. *What background and experience do you have to do the job?*

3. *What additional training do you need to achieve the opportunity you desire?*

4. *Outline your game plan to get the training you need and a timeline to do it!*

Affirmation:

"Thank you Lord for supplying all of my needs and for revealing exciting new career opportunities that will glorify you and lead me to ultimate success and happiness."

Step #4

LOVE Your Brother and Sisters (Co-workers, Business Associates) Whether It's Returned or Not

"Accept one another, then, just as Christ accepted you, in order to bring praise to God."
Romans 15:7 (NIV)

". . . Let every man be swift to hear, slow to speak, slow to wrath."
James 1:19b

"A Rude Awakening"

I can recall a few times throughout my career when my spiritual principles, patience and temper were severely tested while dealing with difficult peers. My 6 year tenure as a Corporate Events Planner, although rewarding for the most part, was not devoid of peer pressures, heated confrontations and unexpected challenges from time to time.

The positive aspects of the job far outweighed any negative experiences I can remember. After all, I was earning a pretty good salary with a flexible work schedule and eating catered food *everyday!* As an Events Planner, I was required to project a positive attitude and professional image on behalf of my company at all times. I planned, hosted and actively supported daily meetings in our Customer Demonstration Center where we hosted guests from all over the world. In addition, I served as the official timekeeper, catering coordinator and onsite administrative and technical support specialist for each customer event.

I was so excited and about my new career opportunity that I failed to notice that at least one member of my new peer group was not as eager to work with me as the others. I had interviewed with each staff member prior to accepting the position. I was told by Mr. Macatee, the Director, that I had been the unanimous choice for the job. However, shortly after my arrival to Team Customer Demonstration Center, I got the feeling that not everyone was happy I was selected for the job. *Stan,* one of the senior members of the presentation staff, made no secret that he wasn't ready to accept me as the replacement for the previous events planner, who was a really good friend of his. He seemed to completely overlook the fact that the former Events Manager had *voluntarily* moved on to another position of her choice.

In the first few months of my new position, I was trying desperately to develop an effective routine for scheduling, planning and orchestrating successful customer events. I would sometimes solicit Stan's advice on how the day's agenda should flow to ensure maximum success for an event. I was told, during my brief training with the former Events Planner, Donna, that Stan was a good source to work with to construct meeting agendas. Stan had a wealth of knowledge on a number of products our company offered and he knew how the order of the presentations on these services should flow to construct a sensible agenda. However, I found that Stan often appeared too busy to talk to me or had little to say that was any help in my planning efforts.

Once Stan started picking apart the agendas I created in front of my other peers, I knew there was a problem with our relationship. I also started to hear derogatory comments he had made to other members of our team about my event planning practices. Initially, I tried not to take Stan's comments to heart. After all, I had been warned from other members of our staff that Stan could be quite abrasive and somewhat of a bully at times. I began to think he was just uptight with his job, needed a vacation, a change of occupation or all three! I did the best I could to overlook Stan's unfounded, negative attitude towards me so I could focus on my events planning responsibilities more closely.

Ironically, when Stan was in front of our customers, he was the jovial, pleasing presentation professional. His distinctive southern drawl was appealing to many of our guest, especially those who lived outside of the South. Most customers loved him! He often told stories about his experiences in business and shared humorous anecdotes he'd either heard about or read about throughout his career.

Stan was *the* product expert of a unique service our company offered to the marketplace called VPN (Virtual Private Network). Although I would schedule him to talk about VPN as requested by our customers, Stan would spend at least half of his allotted time talking about *his personal triumphs in business!* Sometimes, customers enjoyed his stories. Sometimes, they didn't! On most occasions, our customers where more interested in hearing about how our company's services could help them serve their customers more efficiently and economically.

One particular day, our company hosted a small number of executives visiting with us from another Fortune 100 corporation. The company would be awarding millions of dollars of business to either our company or one of our competitors largely based on what they heard throughout the day during their visit with us.

The day had started early and the agenda was packed with presentations on at least 10 different products we offered. The agenda also featured a special presentation from one of our senior sales executives during a catered working lunch. The highlight of the day was our prospects' viewing of at least five live product demonstrations of our company's capabilities. It was not the kind of day where we could afford to fall behind schedule. Our guests had very tight flight connections back to their respective homes shortly after the end of the last presentation. With all of this under consideration, I sent a series of reminder voicemail messages out to all presenters, including the secretary of the President of Sales. I reminded them of our customers' objectives for the day and stressed how critical it was that we stay on schedule to ensure the customers received all the information they requested to make an informed decision that would hopefully favor our company winning their business.

I ran into Stan early on the morning of the event and asked if he had any questions regarding the voicemail message I had left for him earlier. He said he had no idea what I was talking about. It was obvious that he had not listened to his voicemail messages prior to the start of the event. I took a brief moment to emphasize *again* the importance of staying on schedule throughout the event as our guests had extremely tight return flight connections immediately after the last presentation of the day. Stan seemed to take my comments personally—in a negative way. He seemed to think I was picking on him. He murmured something I couldn't quite understand then, quickly walked passed me disappearing down a long, narrow hallway. He never stopped nor slowed down to question or clarify my comments. I said a quick prayer, *"Lord, give me patience!"* and proceeded to the lobby to greet our guests.

The morning went smoothly, according to plan. When the time arrived for Stan to give his forty-five minute presentation on VPN, he was the only thing standing between the successful completion of the days' agenda and our guests return flights' home. Once I was sure our customers were seated comfortably for the start of Stan's presentation, I set the digital countdown clock in the back of the room to '45' minutes and motioned for Stan to *begin.*

I then pressed the button on the digital clock to begin the final countdown to our last presentation of the day. Stan took a quick glance at the clock as it quickly displayed to "44" minutes remaining. As I turned to leave the room, I could hear Stan plunging into his usual slow, deliberate introduction. I was hoping he would speed things up for the sake of ending on time. I used the time during Stan's presentation to check on our guests' limousine and flight arrangements and other last minute tasks, prior to the end of our event.

About thirty minutes after Stan's presentation started, I visited our monitor room to see how things were going. The monitor room consisted of a wall of television monitors which were connected to closed-circuit cameras mounted in the corners of each or our five presentation areas located throughout our demonstration center. When I switched the monitor to the Interactive Demonstration Area (known as the IDA), I was shocked at what I saw! Stan was still on his introduction. He hadn't even begun his presentation. I could tell from the body language of the customers that they were growing weary of Stan's one-sided rhetoric! It must have crossed their minds that making their tight flight connections may not happen if Stan persisted much longer.

I hurried to the presentation room to see if there was anything I could do to get "Stan-the-Run-away-Train" back on track. As I entered the room, our guests appeared relieved to see me. Stan, however, continued to talk as though he hadn't seen me standing in the back of the room trying desperately to get his attention. As he eventually paused for a moment to collect his thoughts, I used that moment to try to tactfully interrupt his 'soap-box, self-indulging' speech. Pleading on behalf of our guests, I voiced my concern regarding the little time we had left on the clock. Considering the time, I asked our guests what they wanted to do—allow Stan to continue his presentation until completion or reschedule his presentation to another time so they wouldn't risk missing their flights?

The customers looked pleased and relieved that I was making an attempt to get their agenda back on track. However, Stan appeared to take my forced interruption like a slap in the face! With little warning, he angrily yelled at me, "You don't tell me how to do my presentation! I'll do this presentation as I see fit, *I'm* the presentation professional, not *you!*" The customers were obviously shocked at Stan's unwarranted outburst. I was both humiliated and embarrassed for our guests, their account team, company and for Stan. The fire in Stan's voice and the anger in his eyes chilled my bones for a brief moment. It was obvious at this point that his hostility was totally directed at *me.* Almost immediately, our guests' account manager spoke up in my defense and thanked me for being so time conscious. He then encouraged Stan to show them a few brief demonstrations using the service coupled with a very brief explanation for the customer. The account manager said he would provide whatever additional information his customers needed on the service during a follow-up visit to their offices in the near future.

I guess Stan must have realized how unprofessional he must have sounded, for, he quickly began to make light of his outburst. He explained that his only desire was to ensure our customers heard all of the unique advantages of our service. We all wanted that too—about an hour ago! Stan's futile attempt at doing damage control was a little too late for our customers and for me. He had managed, single-handedly, to put a major blemish on an otherwise flawless day.

Once Stan agreed to wrap up his presentation in the next few minutes, I left the room again. This time, I wanted, no, I *needed* to find a quiet place to pray! I found a quiet, deserted stairwell to quickly collect my thoughts and to calm myself down. I called on God to give me strength to move beyond this humiliating incident and to focus on making the remainder of the event as pleasant as possible for our customers. As He had done so many times in the past, God gave me the peace and strength I needed to see the event through to the end. I prayed that He would take away the anger I was feeling toward Stan for his actions. He replaced my anger with compassion and a forgiving spirit. I knew that I would have to face Stan eventually to discuss what had happened.

Immediately following his presentation, Stan disappeared and was nowhere to be found for the remainder of the afternoon. I later learned that he had made a beeline to our group manager's office to talk to him about what had happened. He wanted to put his unique spin on the day's event so he wouldn't appear to be at fault in his actions. He actually told my manager that I had rudely interrupted his presentation as he was trying to wrap up his speech to our guests!

When I was summoned into my manager's office later that day to tell my version of the story, I decided to down-play the incident so that Stan would not get in trouble. I said that perhaps my timing was a little off when I interrupted Stan. I told my manager that my main objectives were to successfully complete the day's agenda and get the customer out the door in time to catch their flights. I didn't want to prolong this uncomfortable situation nor give Stan any more ammunition for his mounting hostility toward me. My manager encouraged me to talk to Stan to discuss how we could work more amicably together going forward.

God gave me the courage and will to seek Stan out to discuss our little rift and to find a way to make peace. I refused to be bullied or intimidated by someone for doing what I perceived was right. Arranging a meeting with Stan was no easy feat. He managed to avoid me for at least two days following the event. I was beginning to think he was purposely avoiding me. On the third day following the incident, I glimpsed Stan moving quickly along a crowded hallway in our building. Before I could catch up with him, he had disappeared via an elevator. Still, I waited patiently for an opportunity to address the uncomfortable working environment that had developed between us. My chance to speak to Stan came later that day. I was in the Executive Lounge of our Customer Demonstration Center, preparing for another customer visit when Stan suddenly entered the room. Perhaps he thought the room was empty, as I made very little noise as I sat quietly at a table, assembling folders of literature for our guests.

So, there we were, finally face to face. For a moment, the silence was deafening as both of us waited for the other to speak. I managed to find the words to break the silence first. I asked Stan if he had a few moments to sit down and talk to me. He reluctantly agreed. I moved away from the table toward the large leather couch. I motioned for Stan to sit down next to me. I started by apologizing to Stan for any discomfort I caused by abruptly interrupting his presentation a few days before. I also commended him as one of the most knowledgeable members of our presentation team. I knew I could learn a lot from him, if only we could get past this awkward incident. Although I was a little nervous at first, it felt much better finally facing Stan as opposed to fearing an inevitable confrontation. Our sitting down and discussing our feelings regarding the incident did far more for improving our working relationship than enlisting the intervention of our manager or the opinions of other members of our team. Stan and I discussed ways we could support each other so we didn't repeat what happened a few days earlier. We agreed we were on the same team and our ultimate goal was to ensure our customers receive positive, timely information regarding the best solutions for their businesses.

Stan and I found some common ground that afternoon to grow and improve our working relationship. Amazingly enough, we soon became good friends. Months later, we were even able to laugh about our rocky start.

Summary:

Establishing healthy, positive interpersonal relationships are some of the biggest challenges we may face in the workplace. We can't always expect our peers to like us because *we* want them to. People often have personal issues and insecurities that have nothing to do with us. Their hidden issues may cause them to react negatively to the people they work with. Although we can't change these individuals, we can continue to treat them with respect and kindness and pray that they will eventually take steps to deal with their personal challenges and correct their negative ways. We can't change these individuals, but *God can*. By constantly lifting these individuals up in prayer, God can transform the most negative, difficult co-worker into a more positive, compassionate, caring one. Until these individuals go through God's amazing transformation, it would be wise to limit your interaction with anyone who may have a negative influence on you and the work you've been empowered to do. Take comfort in the words of Romans 8:31, *"When God is for us, who can be against us!"*

Exercise:

1. *Identify the constant whiners, complainers and/or trouble-makers in your organization?*

2. *What are you willing to do to change yourself or distance yourself from the negative influences of your peers?*

Affirmation:

"I will first seek to understand those who may not agree with my position in life, then to be understood. I will follow the awesome example of Jesus by striving to resolve any conflicts I am faced with in peace, harmony and love."

Step #5

TURN Trials and Tribulations into Triumphs

"Blessed is the man who perseveres under trial, because when he has stood the test, he will receive the crown of life that God has promised to those who love him."
James 1:12 (NIV)

"These things I have spoken unto you, that in me ye might have peace. In the world ye shall have tribulation: But be of good cheer; I have overcome the world."
John 16:33 (NIV)

"Feeling the Fire"

I think that as long as I shall live, I'll never forget Sunday, July 24, 1994. For me, it marked a day of celebration and devastation. I found lots to celebrate that day as God had blessed me to see my thirty-first birthday in great health surrounded by loving family and devoted friends. Most importantly, my husband and I were happily awaiting the arrival of our first-born son. I was seven months pregnant and adjusting to the reality of becoming a new mom in a few short months.

Unfortunately, the happiness and joy of my special day was unexpectedly overshadowed with tragedy. The young thriving greeting card business my husband and I had worked hard to build over a seven year period had literally gone up in flames. To make matters worse, this unfortunate mishap apparently occurred at the hands of an alleged arsonist for reasons we have yet to know.

I'll never forget the phone call I received that Monday morning following the devastating fire. I had been in meetings all morning at another office and was unaware of the devastation to our greeting card business the day before. I checked my voicemail messages to find a rather solemn message from the secretary of our greeting card company. She stated there had been a fire at the office building we shared with our commercial printer and business partners, Barry and Karen Bershad of Plaza Printing. Her only other comment was that I should come to the office as soon as possible.

Since life was going so well for me up to that point, I refused to think the worse had happened until I could gather more facts. I thought our business partner must have neglected repairing the air conditioner I heard one of his employees talking about the week leading up to the fire. Perhaps it had malfunctioned over the weekend. Or, maybe one of the printing presses had overheated.

I was totally unprepared for what I saw as I drove toward the building which once served as my company's corporate headquarters. The fire had caused major structural damage to the outside of the two story green stucco building. So much so, the building had actually split open on the side, exposing the contents of the first and second floors. All of the windows on the front of the building were blown out. Firemen wrapped the building in yellow caution tape to keep spectators at bay.

Through my dismay, I noticed at least two police officers standing on the corner in front of the charred building directing traffic. A number of drivers and pedestrians moved slowly passed the building trying to get a closer look at the damage. What was most disheartening was the expressions on the faces of the Plaza Printing employees who had reported to work as scheduled with no clue a fire had even happened. Imagine their surprise to find their workplace totally gutted, destroyed by fire and their financial stability and careers in jeopardy.

As I looked for a place to park on the crowded street behind the building, the first person I noticed in the crowd gathered around the building was Karen Bershad. Karen was the co-owner of Plaza Printing and the wife of my business partner, Barry Bershad. Karen and I embraced tightly and took a brief moment to share a cry over our losses. Karen and Barry had spent over 30 years building their small family-owned printing business. In 1993, my husband, Rodric, and I accepted a unique offer to make Plaza Printing our business partner. The purpose of our partnership was to mass-produce and distribute my unique line of greeting cards to retail stores and outlets throughout the United States.

Up until the fire, our company had experienced significant success and publicity in the marketplace. Our partnership with Plaza Printing appeared to be working out just fine. The Bershads and their Plaza Printing team provided administrative support and printing services for our business as well as order fulfillment and warehousing. In public, I was the spokesperson and face of our company. Behind the scenes, my primary responsibilities included creative design, public relations, marketing and sales. Together, we had successfully distributed our product line to over 250 retail customers nationwide. The list of customers grew daily.

Rodric and I cherished the thought of eventually leaving our corporate jobs to focus of growing our small greeting card business to a world-class operation. The fire, however, put an abrupt halt to our dreams for the moment. Not only was the building totally destroyed by the fire, but all of our inventory, original artwork, business records including customer files and computer databases were also destroyed. At the time, I felt like I had lost *everything!*

As the news of the fire spread, we began receiving phone calls from concerned business allies and customers expressing their regrets and condolences. I felt numb and confused. It was as though a part of me had died in the fire. After all, I had passionately created our greeting card business from my love of writing and drawing. I had nurtured my craft, researched it, tested it and initially painted each and every card design by hand. Once convinced I had a viable product line, I searched high and low to find a commercial printer to mass-produce my greeting card collection.

I had asked God, "*Please send me someone to help make my vision a reality.*" God sent Barry and Karen Bershad. Not only did the couple agree to print my greeting card designs, they offered to become our business partners to share the risk and rewards of launching our exciting new business.

I questioned, *"How could this awful thing happen to us after being so close to realizing our dreams?"* Then I thought, "*Why not us?"* We weren't so different from anyone else who had experienced unexpected trials and tribulations. Trials are inevitable as long as we're 'living' in this world. Our challenge was, would we let this tragedy help define our eventual success or foretell our future failure. Rodric and I decided that no matter the outcome, we wouldn't quit! Our dream to build a successful, inspiring greeting card company to share with the world was stronger than the urge to give up and quit.

I sought God's guidance almost constantly throughout this ordeal. I knew that an event as devastating as the fire had to have some underlying lesson or purpose to it. My daily affirmation was, *"God is so good. I know He will ensure something good comes from this tragedy."* I knew God had another direction for my career, my life, but what? I didn't find out God's plan for my future right away. As a matter of fact, it wasn't until a year or so *after* the fire and the birth of our first-born son that I started to realize God's plans for the resurrection of our entrepreneurial dreams.

Unfortunately, we received no financial compensation from our former business partner or their insurance claims for our losses in the fire. The final figure of our losses was in excess of ***$70,000***. Although we thought our business assets had adequate coverage under the printer's comprehensive insurance policy, it appeared the insurance company was not going to pay off on the bulk of the policy. For reasons I'm still unsure of, the printer's multi-million dollar policy was denied. As a result, our printer was forced into early retirement. My husband and I were left to contemplate our future in business with no viable means of financing or continuing our entrepreneurial endeavors.

We were left with little more than the ideas, passion and desires that initially launched our greeting card company. We did, however, retrieve a printout of a list of former customers from the rubble of the printer's partially burned office building. I asked God to use this experience to direct, lead and orchestrate the rebirth of our business as *He* desired. Being forced to start over, I found it much easier this time around to turn *total control* of our business over to God.

Almost a year after the fire, I received a rather surprising phone call from a reporter with *Inc. Magazine*, a nationally distributed magazine targeting entrepreneurs and businesses. The reporter was requesting an interview with me for an upcoming issue of a newsletter for BellSouth Communications Company *(currently AT&T)*. Inc. Magazine had contracted with BellSouth to write their quarterly newsletter targeting small business customers throughout the Southeast.

The reporter mentioned he had read an article about our business about a year before and was interested in doing a follow up story on the progress of my partnership with the printer. Further, he stated how courageous and clever we were to partner with a larger, more established business to produce my greeting card line. He said most start-up small business owners are usually hesitant to let others share their visions for risk of their ideas being stolen or drastically altered. After asking him a few questions to establish his authenticity, I was finally convinced the voice on the other end of the phone was indeed a legitimate reporter for Inc. Magazine. He obviously had no idea we had suffered a major setback in our business just one year prior to his call.

I spent the next several minutes bringing the reporter up to speed on everything that had transpired since the last positive article he'd read about our company. In short, I told him the fire put us out of business, literally, overnight. We would have to start all over again from scratch with little financial resources and no printing partner like before. Surprised by the news, the reporter began asking me a series of probing questions regarding the unfortunate demise of my once promising business. He seemed most impressed when I stated with conviction that somehow, someway, someday, God would help us find a way to revive our greeting card business. He was most moved by my display of unshakable faith and my confidence that somehow God would help us rebuild our business. I told him that the rebirth of our business was quietly and strategically being orchestrated by God. *God has a **100%** success record for business revivals and turnarounds.*

The reporter was so inspired by my testimony that he successfully appealed to his editor to write a feature story about our company entitled, *"The Anatomy of a Rebound"*. Our tragedy was hailed as a promising triumph and the cover story in BellSouth's summer '95 edition of their ***'Small Business Connection'*** newsletter. The article featured a color picture of me displaying several of my best-selling greeting card designs. The newsletter was distributed to over 215,000 of BellSouth's small business clients throughout the Southeast. The positive, *free* publicity and exposure the article gave our company, was worth well over ***$250,000***!

The article was a source of inspiration for a number of small business owners throughout the Southeast who read it. Not long after the newsletter was distributed, we began receiving positive, encouraging phone calls from small business owners throughout the country. Through the encouragement of our small business peers, my husband and I knew we had to find a way to get our product line back into the marketplace. We knew that it was just a matter of time before God revealed the details of our comeback to us.

In the meantime, we took inventory of all our financial assets to determine what funds we had to invest in the revival of our business. We reviewed our savings account. It was bleak at best. With the expenses of having a new baby onboard, we didn't have nearly enough money saved to pay to have all of my greeting card designs reprinted. The solution—we decided to take a second loan out on Rodric's SUV to get part of the money to reprint some of the best-selling designs from my collection. The loan from our bank and a generous loan from my father-in-law provided us with enough start-up capital to reprint our cards. We then tried to borrow money from a large, commercial bank for other business-related needs such as greeting card racks, brochures, computer, printer, business stationary, etc. However, since we could not produce previous financial statements that were lost in the fire, our loan application was eventually denied. Nonetheless, God has a way of opening a window when a door is suddenly closed.

Through the Small Business Development Center of Kennesaw State University located in Kennesaw, Georgia, we were introduced to a wonderful individual who happened to be an investment banker. His company primarily searched for new business opportunities to invest in and advise for maximum success. This gentleman was known in the business field as, *"an angel investor"*. Immediately, I knew God had a hand in bringing us together. After a few meetings with him, our 'Angel' investor loaned us the remaining funds we needed to successfully re-launch our business.

Rodric and I decided to incorporate our business this time around for additional protection. When our attorney asked us to assign officers for the corporation, I knew that the only name to go under the title of CEO was ***'GOD.'*** As a symbolic gesture of our commitment to make 'glorifying God' a #1 priority in our business, we left space blank next to the title of CEO on our incorporation paperwork. I was named President of our new company. Rodric was named Vice President and Secretary of our company. And, my cousin Gerard, who was a practicing Certified Public Accountant in the Atlanta area, was named our Treasurer. For their wisdom, encouragement and financial assistance, my father-in-law and our *angel investor* were offered and accepted positions on our company's Board of Directors.

Glory to God, by the summer of 1996, we were back in business distributing our inspirational line of greeting cards to stores near and far! We were able to re-capture business from many of the retailers that had carried our greeting card collection before. A special blessing that really helped us get successfully re-launched was an order from a past client to place our cards in at least 142 of their stores throughout the US! Shortly thereafter, we were approved for at least two other major retailers and a host of gifts and specialty stores primarily in the Southeast.

In September 1997, almost a year after re-entering the marketplace—our company was honored as an *"Outstanding Atlanta Business" at the Atlanta Business League's Annual Awards Luncheon*. I was most humbled and honored to be nominated by peers of the Atlanta business community to receive this prestigious award. During my acceptance speech, I boldly glorified God's resurrecting power to bring our company back from the ashes to achieve greater feats in business and life!

Summary:

During his sermon one Sunday, I recall my pastor defining the word ***'fear'*** as, *'**f**alse **e**vidence **a**ppearing **r**eal'*. Yet, many of us are guilty of letting *fear* or *'a lack of faith'* block us from achieving our biggest dreams and goals in life. Christian or non-Christian, churched or not, as long as we live on planet Earth, we will be faced with trials and tribulations. However, if we consistently practice feeding our faith and starving our fears through prayer and meditation, God can move more swiftly and deliberately to guide us to our triumphs in life. We must have faith that he will NEVER abandon us—even when our dreams may go up in flames or friends, family and co-workers may walk away. He will deliver us from whatever challenges we may be facing in HIS time which is ALWAYS on time! We must be still, be faithful and thank him in advance for our deliverance. God is ready, willing and able to see us through the storms of life. He just asks that we continue to be obedient to his word and BELIEVE!

Exercise:

1. *If you had no fear of failure, what top three dreams/goals would you like to achieve in the near future?*

2. *Write down your goals in detail and lift them up in prayer to GOD. Share them with at least two of your closest Christian friends and ask them to pray with you to make your dreams a reality.*

Affirmation:

"God, you are the CEO of my life. I will risk EVERYTHING to follow you. For through you, JOY and abundant BLESSINGS are mine today, tomorrow and for ETERNITY."

Step #6

LIVE Each Day to the Fullest While in Pursuit of Your Dreams

"Therefore take no thought for the morrow for the morrow shall take thought for the things of itself. Sufficient unto the day is the evil thereof."
Matthew 6:34 (KJV)

"What a Friend's Dying Taught Me about Living"

As long as we live, we are destined to encounter people in life who will leave lasting impressions on us either positively or negatively. Throughout my career, I've enjoyed working with a few extremely special individuals who have blessed my life just by knowing them. Some of them were in my life for only a short while—perhaps to serve a specific purpose in God's master plan for my career. Others, I still keep in touch with from time to time—although the bond may not be as strong as it once was. And still, there are those very special few folks I would love to have connected with for a while longer, but, God called them home suddenly to be with Him. In these instances, I'm only left with fond memories of the times we shared once shared together.

A dear friend of mine that I felt I lost too soon was my former co-worker, *Jennifer*. Jennifer lost her battle with cancer in the fall of 1996. At the height of our working relationship and evolving friendship, Jennifer and I discovered we had a lot in common. To start, we were both mothers of young sons. We both enjoyed using our gifts of creativity to collaborate on exciting marketing projects. And, we both enjoyed writing and being co-conspirators in the planning of our office parties and other fun team-building initiatives!

Jennifer and I initially had the opportunity to work together in my former role as an Events Manager at a leading telecommunications company. Jennifer was the department secretary. Although to some in my department, the role of secretary meant glorified *paper pusher* and *phone monitor*, I knew differently. Jennifer was indeed the *glue* that held our department together. One of the most memorable characteristics of Jennifer's personality was her great sense of humor. She adored the bizarre humor captured in Gary Larson's *'Far Side'* comic strip. She would clip and paste the latest Far Side comic on a special wall near her desk for her peers to enjoy on any given day

Jennifer loved to have fun! She had a passion for playing the game of tennis. I would often observe her making a quick exit from the employee parking garage in the evenings to attend her weekly tennis matches. Sometimes when I close my eyes, I can still see Jen's long mane of thick curly brunette hair blowing in the wind from her blue and white Chrysler convertible. She was passionate and committed to her tennis dates and rarely missed a match for work or anything else!

Jennifer was indeed a *'perfectionist'*. She believed in doing things right the first time, because having to do it over could cut into her tennis time! My co-workers and I admired the tools she created for us such as the departmental procedures manual, informational memos and carefully planned team training sessions. Jennifer left little room for mistakes or errors in her work. I found EVERY Jennifer Smith document or project to be accurate, neat and complete. I guess that's why, after ten years of serving as a company secretary, Jennifer was offered to a position of promotion in our company's Marketing Department. Her new responsibilities involved the creation of quality company literature, presentations and special projects for our customer demonstration center. It was a role perfectly suited for Jennifer's talents and she wasted no time putting everything she had into it!

Although Jennifer had little experience working on any computer graphics or literature design software, she was quite eager to learn. She spent hours observing more proficient literature design experts on our team in an effort to improve her creative skills. Jennifer was often the last person to leave the office in the evening while working on improving her performance as a literature design expert. When she wasn't working on a critical design project, Jennifer and I would sometimes have lunch together to get caught up on what was going on in our respective lives. On a few occasions, Jennifer and I would discuss the possibility of collaborating on a series of children's books. She was an excellent writer and I was also a good writer and a pretty good artist. Jennifer and I decided to co-write the stories and I would be the primary illustrator for our exciting new line of children's books. We often discussed other jobs or careers we would love to have if our jobs were suddenly eliminated. Little did we know we would be faced with a corporate lay-off that would have a profound effect on both of our lives.

We were actually notified about a year in advance that our company's Southeast marketing department would be moved from Atlanta, GA to Dallas, TX by the spring 1996. Initially, Jennifer, I and many of our peers were in denial about the news of possibly losing our jobs. Among ourselves, we questioned our company's upper management to up-root and move such a professional, productive, close-knit group of individuals to *TEXAS?!?* Many of my team members quickly confirmed that they WOULD NOT be making the move to Texas because of personal reasons.

Unfortunately, we found ourselves attaching human feelings and characteristics to an inanimate entity—*our jobs!* The *corporation* had made a business decision based on its overall objectives for future growth and expansion. Although its business decision had a major impact on me and my peers *personally,* it was just business. The good news, we were each promised a job in our new Dallas marketing offices, if we made the decision to relocate. However, of the thirty or so individuals left in the Atlanta-based marketing department, only two (2) decided to actually relocate to Dallas. The rest of us were left behind to contemplate our futures and anticipate the inevitable closing of our Atlanta-based marketing office.

Although company management had promised the Atlanta marketing team continued work doing 'special projects' until the Dallas marketing office opened in April 1996, they had changed their minds by December 1995. With only ten Atlanta-based marketers left, we were called into an abrupt meeting with Human Resources during the first week of December 1995. The Human Resources representative informed us that our last day with the company would be in two weeks—during the week of Christmas! Imagine how crushed many of us felt who were still grappling with the idea of unemployment being a reality in the spring. Jennifer seemed especially devastated by the news. She wanted us to rally together to force the corporation to live up to its promise of assigning us special projects until the spring of 1996. However, legally, there was nothing any of us could do except deal with the decision that had been made by moving on as quickly as possible to other promising career opportunities OR by re-considering a move to the new marketing headquarters in Dallas!

It seemed like Jennifer's life started a downhill spiral from that day forward. While me and most of my remaining marketing peers spent the following weeks setting up job interviews with other employer prospects or researching going into business for ourselves, Jennifer continued to work diligently on completing the 'busy work' the company had previously assigned to her. She appeared to be in deep denial regarding the fast-approaching end to her 12+ year career with the company. Unfortunately, her personal life wasn't doing much better than her career. Jennifer had shared with me and a few other co-workers that she was contemplating a divorce and she was also dealing with some rather distressful behavioral challenges of her young son. I could sense that my dear friend was under a great deal of stress and pressure—both personally and professionally.

Jennifer had no idea *what* she wanted to do once her job ended. Although she didn't see it that way, Jennifer was one of the more fortunate marketing employees. Because of her 12+ year tenure with the company, Jennifer would receive at least 6 months of severance pay plus benefits beginning on our official release date. Her severance compensation package was at least twice as much as that of her peers. The majority of the remaining marketers had only been with the company for 5 years or less. Instead of being thankful for six months of uninterrupted pay and benefits, Jennifer spent most of her time worrying about what to do once she didn't have a corporate office to report to each day. For the first time in a long time, Jennifer would be forced to spend time dealing with those areas of her personal life she had neglected for so long.

I attempted to reach out to Jennifer on several occasions after we said our good-byes on the last day of working together in our Atlanta marketing offices. Unfortunately, Jennifer withdrew from her former co-workers and friends shortly thereafter. Perhaps pulling away was the only way she knew to cope with the trials she was facing and the fear she was feeling regarding her future. When she stopped returning my calls, the only thing I could do was pray for Jennifer and her family.

In the days and months that followed, I asked God to help my former peers find rich, rewarding careers according to His purpose for their lives. A few individuals found other jobs almost immediately. A couple of them moved to other states to pursue other career options. And, a few of us decided to take the entrepreneurial plunge and start business on our own. The remaining members of our team decided to take some time off to give much needed attention to their households and families. I was blessed to be hired back at the company within a few short months in a newly created marketing management position in another Atlanta-based division of our company.

Although Jennifer and I lost contact for a short while after our work together had ended, I still thought about her often. Prior to our last days working together, I had loaned her some of my favorite motivational tapes to help her focus on a positive plan for her future. I also shared powerful biblical scriptures she could use that had given me strength and comfort throughout my career. Jennifer told me once, although she didn't know what she wanted to do in her life after Corporate America, she felt that I would make an *awesome motivational speaker!*

By the summer of 1996, Jennifer's life had taken a turn for the worse! Although she still didn't know what she wanted to do professionally in the months following the closing of our Atlanta-based marketing department, Jennifer still actively pursued her love of playing tennis. One day, while engaging in a tennis match with a friend of hers, Jennifer suddenly collapsed on the tennis court. She was immediately rushed to the hospital to determine what was wrong. The initial diagnosis—one of her lungs had collapsed. Upon running further tests on her to determine the cause, doctors found traces of cancer in Jennifer's lungs. The devastating news of Jennifer's tragic ailment brought members of the former marketing department back together again. We rallied around our friend and her family in an effort to ease their pain and support them any way we could. We all prayed for a miraculous cure for our dear friend Jennifer. We did everything we could to encourage her and to give her a will to fight the toughest battle of her life.

I recall visiting Jennifer at her home in between treatments for her cancer. The cancer had progressed throughout her body and had spread to her brain. Although Jennifer and I had talked on the phone a few times over the months prior to her collapse, I had not physically seen her since the last day we worked together. My friend and former co-worker, Phil Calvert and I decided we would go together to visit Jennifer one fall afternoon. Phil had worked very closely with Jennifer for at least three years in our former marketing department. He was the graphics guru that taught Jennifer most of what she knew about computer-based graphics design and literature production. The two of them shared a lot of fond memories together. They also shared the same witty sense of humor. I felt like, if anyone can bring a smile to Jennifer's face and help her forget her challenges for a while, *Phil could!*

When Jennifer answered the door upon our arrival to her home, I was literally *shocked* by the changes to her once statuesque appearance. Jennifer was almost six feet tall, very attractive and her trademark had been her long, thick locks of bushy, brunette hair. However, the Jennifer standing before us in the open doorway was slightly hunched over, quite frail-looking with all signs of her long, flowing mane of hair *gone!* Instead, Jennifer donned a bald, red, radiation-treated scalp which totally altered the memory I had of the person I once worked with. We could tell Jennifer was a little self-conscious and irritated by the loss of her hair, because throughout our visit with her, she kept touching, rubbing and scratching her scalp.

Once inside her home, Jennifer invited us to have a seat on the sofa in her living room while she lay down on a hospital-style bed that had been set up for her in the middle of the room. Jennifer seemed to sense that Phil and I were struggling trying to find the right words to comfort her. So, in true Jennifer style, she broke the silence with a joke! Jennifer told us a key advantage to going bald is, *'you don't have to worry about BAD HAIR DAYS anymore!'* The cancer may have physically altered her appearance, but our dear friend Jennifer had not lost her witty sense of humor. On a roll, Jennifer then told Phil, he could probably try out some of his old jokes on her and she would probably laugh at them, because the cancer had robbed her of a lot of her memory. For the remainder of our visit with her, Jennifer, Phil and I relived some of our most memorable experiences working together and talked about the new memories we would make together once Jennifer conquered her bout with cancer.

For the remainder of the time we spent together that day, Jennifer appeared more optimistic and positive than usual. Jennifer had never been an openly spiritual or religious person, however, I heard my friend reference her love and relationship with Jesus on more than one occasion throughout our visit. My friend had finally found salvation and wasn't afraid to share it! My heart was filled with joy as I realized that Jennifer and I were truly *sisters* in Christ!

Prior to our departure from Jennifer's home, Phil gave her a few motivational books to read during her ongoing treatments and to aid in her eventual recovery from cancer. Because of the rapid progression of the cancer, Jennifer admitted that she would not be able to read the books because her vision had been severely compromised. It was difficult for her to focus on reading small type for an extended period of time. I offered to come back to visit with her in the upcoming week to read to her. Jennifer was ecstatic as she graciously accepted my offer. I still carry a vivid picture in my memory of Jennifer standing on her front porch waving good-bye to Phil and me as we backed out of her driveway following our wonderful visit with her. She stood there smiling and waving at us as she yelled, "*I love you guys!*" We yelled back, '*We love you too!*'

Regretfully, Jennifer and I were unable to keep our reading date the following week. Jennifer's condition took a turn for the worse and she had to be rushed back to the hospital because of cancer-related complications. A few days later, our dear friend Jennifer was dead. Although I had lost my dear friend, former co-worker and sister-in-Christ, the world had lost a truly talented, gifted woman with so much passion and potential! So much of Jennifer's life had been spent perfecting her assignments on her job, devoting her time and talents to her employer and sacrificing her personal time with family and friends to achieve corporate goals. Jennifer did her work to the very best of her ability and for that I will always admire her strong work ethics. However, those things she aspired to do to achieve more meaning and purpose in her life—such as spending more quality time with her young son and husband, writing a new witty line of children's books and starting her own corporate events and graphic design company—will never be realized,

The ultimate lesson I learned from my dear friend Jennifer's life is, *'we each have a finite amount of time to make a positive mark on the world.'* Our days are uniquely numbered to make positive contributions to mankind, to spend quality time with family and friends, to work on achieving our goals and to fulfill God's purpose for our lives. If we defer our dreams indefinitely, or give up on them, we may never realize the satisfaction and joy of completing a positive, purpose-filled life.

Summary:

Life is not always fair, pleasant or predictable. Bad things DO happen to good people and tomorrow is certainly not promised to any of us. However, there are still things we can do—starting TODAY—to ensure we make a positive difference in the world. We can utilize our spiritual gifts to create an empowering product, service or business for others to enjoy long after we're gone. Instead of feeling sorry for the hand that life has dealt to us thus far, we can vow to live life to the fullest with the hand that we have. God has a unique assignment for each of us. Seek his guidance and mercy in whatever situation you find yourself and HE will make a way for you out of no way!

Exercise:

1. *List the top three challenges or trials you're facing right now.*

2. *Appeal to God in prayer to help you endure or overcome these challenges by solving or removing them from your life.*

3. *What one (1) thing have you been putting off that can positively change your life or those around you?*

4. *Draft a thirty (30) day game plan to complete or make significant progress in achieving your goal(s) in life. Persist until your goal is complete!*

Affirmation:

"God, thank you for the fire, focus and determination to complete the work you have assigned me to do. I will glorify your name and positively impact the lives of others for as long as I am living!"

Step #7

INCREASE Your Faith, Focus and Follow-through to Increase Your Success

". . . For verily I say unto you, if you have faith as a grain of mustard seed, ye shall say unto this mountain, remove hence to yonder place; And it shall remove; and nothing shall be impossible unto you."
Matthew 17:20 (KJV)

"For we walk by faith, not by sight."
2 Corinthians 5:7

"A Tale of Two Giants"

Throughout my 10+ years as an employee in Corporate America, I had often dreamed of leaving the hustle and bustle of corporate life behind to launch a successful business enterprise of my own. Initially, my dream was to build a unique greeting cards and gifts manufacturing and distribution company. In an effort to achieve my dreams, I started a small greeting cards company on a part-time basis while working full-time as a Marketing Manager for a Fortune 500 telecommunications company. My initial product line consisted of hand-painted, custom greeting cards for family, friends and co-workers. I later developed a comical cast of four fun-loving cartoon characters to feature in a unique all-occasion greeting card collections entitled, *'Belle's Boutique.'* I spent almost five years testing my greeting card designs in various small specialty stores, craft festivals and industry trade shows primarily in the Atlanta area. I also administered at least one marketing survey to a class of marketing students at Clark Atlanta University. My focus was to see if college students would be interested in purchasing my line of greeting cards. All the data I collected CONFIRMED that college students would definitely patronize my line if it was readily available in the marketplace.

My husband and I spent the better part of 1996 seeking financing for our new business venture, then, getting inventory and product brochures produced. We had the product, we knew there was a target market for it, however, we were in need of an effective distribution channel. Our goal was to get our products to retailers and ultimately, into the hands of consumers as quickly as possible.

To solve our distribution dilemma, I decided to recruit an ambitious group of women to serve as independent distributors for my company. Their sales territory was initially the Metro Atlanta area. However, since most of the women had full-time jobs and couldn't focus on sales for my company until the weekend, sales were few and far between from the group as a whole. We could only afford to pay our team on a commission basis, so, if they didn't sell, they didn't get paid. Since I was also working full-time on my corporate job, I knew the only way our new company could survive is if I could eventually leave my corporate job to focus on growing our new business full-time. My husband and I discussed the financial sacrifices we would have to make to ensure my successful transition from a middle manager at a Fortune 500 company to President of a start-up business enterprise.

Rodric and I determined that when I was successful in confirming at least two major retail chain stores with a total of up to 250 store locations, I could leave my corporate job to run our greeting card distribution company full-time. This base of accounts would provide me with the means to replace the income from my corporate job as well as the financing our company needed to grow and expand our product line and service territory.

Initially, I targeted the top two grocery store chains in the Southeast, Kroger Stores and Publix Super Markets, Inc. At the time, Kroger had approximately 200 store locations throughout the Metro Atlanta area and was known as the #1 grocery store chain in Atlanta. Florida-based Publix Super Markets, Inc. was holding down the #2 slot, but gaining ground quickly on Kroger's long-standing dominance throughout Georgia. I decided to contact Kroger first regarding the distribution of my greeting card collection—since they were the top grocery retailer in the area. When I was finally able to get the Kroger's local greeting card buyer on the phone to introduce my new greeting card collection, he suggested that I make an appointment to share my product line with him in person. I scheduled a meeting through the buyer's secretary for two weeks out. I used my extensive corporate marketing communications to create a colorful, comprehensive, formal PowerPoint presentation on my company.The presentation featured our company's mission statement, a summary of our product offer, service and distribution strategy and the benefits of offering our line to Kroger customers.

On the day of my highly-anticipated meeting with the Kroger buyer, I rolled out of my bed shortly before the alarm sounded to pray to God for favor for a positive, productive meeting! I then left the overall success of the meeting in God's extremely capable hands. I proceeded to claim my victory in business—*in Jesus name!* I arrived to the Kroger Regional Buying Office about thirty minutes early. I took the elevator up to the buying office, checked in at the receptionist's desk and took the first available seat in a waiting room packed with other sales reps and aspiring business owners. Like me, I'm sure many of them were hoping to confirm a lucrative order from their respective Kroger buyer.

When my buyer's secretary eventually entered the waiting room to invite me to my buyer's office for our meeting, I quickly picked up my briefcase of sales tools and greeting card display rack and followed her back to his office. My sales tools included a small corrugated cardboard countertop rack to display my sample cards, a three-ring presentation binder containing my colorful Company Overview, product brochures, order information and samples of a few of my best-selling designs.

After being introduced to my Kroger Buyer, I was allowed a few minutes to set up my display rack and product samples on his extremely clean, uncluttered desk. I then proceeded to provide an inspiring presentation on *WHY* Kroger should carry my savvy, new greeting card collection in their local stores. Upon completion of my presentation, the buyer suggested that we conduct a test of my Valentine's Day greeting card collection in select Kroger stores throughout the Metro Atlanta area. He picked the top five highest volume Kroger Stores in the area for the test market. His goal was to determine if my cards would sell in their stores during one of the busiest times for greeting card sales—*Valentine's Day!* His recommendation wasn't exactly the response I had hoped for, however, it was a step in the right direction for securing a more lucrative order with Kroger in the near future. I had *faith* that our product test would be successful and we would be confirmed as *approved vendors* for Kroger Stores *everywhere!*

We pulled out all the stops for our Kroger Valentine's Day test. Because we had less than two weeks before Valentine's Day, I enlisted the assistance of remaining members of our independent distributor team to work in the stores on Valentine's Day to promote our greeting card collection. The extra level of customer service we provided to frantic, last-minute shoppers on Valentine's Day was just what we needed to stand out from our competitors. The end result, we sold nearly 100% of our cards in all five of the Kroger stores. Our test market was a tremendous success!

In the days following our successful product test with Kroger, I confirmed a follow-up meeting with the buyer to discuss our next steps. He was quite pleased with our sales results and suggested that I complete the paperwork to become an approved Kroger vendor as soon as possible. He directed me to send my completed vendor application and supporting documents to the attention of his secretary. I did everything he asked of me, including acquiring a two million dollar liability insurance policy to cover any potential risks of placing my greeting card racks on the sales floors in Kroger stores. I double-checked every line on the application to ensure I had accurately provided all the information requested. Then, I sent my paperwork to my buyer's office via overnight delivery.

A few days later, I phoned the Kroger Buyer's office to confirm that my paperwork had been successfully received. The Buyer's secretary confirmed that she had indeed received my package the day before and had placed the information on her boss's desk for review. Armed with this positive report, I decided to patiently wait for the buyer to call me to confirm my new status as an APPROVED Kroger vendor! I waited and waited and waited and waited for the buyer to call me—for almost three weeks! Then, I decided to call my buyer to get an update on my vendor application. To my dismay, the Kroger Buyer informed me that he had changed his mind about carrying my greeting card line in his stores. Instead, he had decided to stick with his current greeting card suppliers and forgo adding any new companies to his roster of approved vendors for the time being.

I was literally crushed by the Kroger Buyer's decision! I felt like the momentum I had established through the successful test-market of my product in select Kroger Stores was all but gone with this unexpected news. Once I caught my breath, I began asking the buyer a series of questions in an effort to determine what I could have done differently to get him to do more business with me. *I asked if there was something regarding my product line he didn't like? Was my new vendor application inaccurate or incomplete? Was there something I had said or done to offend him?* The buyer answered *'NO'* to all of the above. In a matter-of-fact tone, the buyer actually complimented my efforts of conducting a successful test-market, providing a heightened level of customer service in their stores during Valentine's Day and my follow-up and professionalism throughout our business trial. Instead, his decision was based on the fact that he already had four approved greeting card suppliers in his stores and he just didn't think he had time or desired to deal with making room for yet another line of cards in his greeting card section. Emotionally, I was quite upset by this unexpected case of 'buyer's remorse'. During the last few minutes of our phone conversation, I was at a loss for words to influence the Kroger Buyer to change his mind in my favor. So, although I didn't agree with his decision NOT to carry my greeting card line in his stores for the immediate future, I ended the call by agreeing to respect his decision and with my commitment to follow up with him again sometime in the future.

'Rejection' is a hard pill to swallow! In my moment of despair, again, I turned to God for guidance. *What now Lord?* I believed so strongly in the merits of my product line and was confident that it filled a unique void in the marketplace. I decided I would NOT let the decision of one buyer end my quest to distribute my product line via major retail outlets. God empowered me with the faith, confidence and determination to keep going, to keep persisting. My next prospect was the #2 grocery store retailer in Atlanta at the time—Publix Super Markets, Inc. Publix was based in Lakeland, Florida—my home state. This savvy grocery retailer had entered the Georgia market in the early 90's and had quickly become Kroger's leading competitor. Publix was also the grocery store chain of choice for my beloved grandmother, *Ms. Ida Mae Herring,* throughout my childhood in the quaint little tourist town of Silver Springs, Florida. I was quite familiar with Publix's culture of outstanding customer service and exceptional in-store cleanliness long before I targeted the company to carry my greeting card collection. The company's friendly, courteous management and staff ensure the company consistently lives up to its famous motto of, *"Publix, where shopping is a pleasure!"*

Convincing the Publix Buyer to do business with my company was no easy feat either. Unaware by me at the time, a member of my independent distributor team had already attempted to sell my greeting card collection to Publix via a solicitation letter sent through the mail. It was no wonder Publix mailed back a short, courteous rejection letter in response to her request. I knew that the only way I stood a chance of getting my product line on the shelves of any major retailer was to request a face-to-face meeting with the appropriate buyer. So, I used the Publix rejection letter as motivation to confirm a meeting with the Publix Buyer. Besides the unauthorized approach of soliciting their business via the US mail, I wanted to discuss why my product line had been rejected and what steps I needed to take to become an approved vendor for Publix. I called the Publix Buyer at their Lakeland, Florida headquarters—to request an in-person meeting. It was during this call that the buyer informed me that the decision to reject my product line wasn't his decision, but the decision of their Atlanta Merchandising Director (AMD). It seems the AMD had decided that another greeting card company wasn't needed in their Atlanta stores at the time. I couldn't believe he was giving me the identical reason that the Kroger buyer had offered for rejecting my product line. However, this time, I was prepared with a more compelling response *WHY* the buyer should reconsider his decision. I quickly shared the results of our successful Kroger Valentine's Day test. I explained how we sold nearly 100% of all the greeting cards we placed in Kroger's five highest volume stores in Metro Atlanta in less than one week! I also explained how we positioned customer service representatives from our company in each store to assist shoppers with picking out their Valentine's cards and gifts and keeping customer traffic flowing throughout the greeting card aisle. Our quality greeting card line coupled with our outstanding customer service support assisted Kroger in maximizing their profits for one of the leading holidays for greeting cards and gifts purchases.

I could tell I had piqued the Publix Buyer's curiosity regarding my product offering as he began to ask more probing questions about my successful test with Kroger, which happened to be Publix's leading competitor in the Atlanta market. I confidently proceeded to give one of the strongest, most compelling explanations to date on WHY my product line would be a great fit for Publix stores and their loyal customer base. At the conclusion of our phone conversation, the Publix Buyer was convinced that he and his peer, the AMD, probably needed to take another look at carrying my product line in their stores. He agreed to contact the AMD on my behalf to encourage him to meet with me in person to discuss the merits of my product line. He recommended that I call the AMD's local office within the week to schedule a face-to-face meeting. I followed his suggestion and reached out to the AMD a few days later.

I was met with yet another challenge in my attempt to persuade the Publix AMD to confirm a meeting with me. This gentleman was not very happy about having to reconsider a FINAL decision he had previously made. When I finally got the ADM on the phone and explained who I was and why I wanted to meet with him, I could sense his voice turn from positive and polite to agitated and angry almost immediately! He was quite bothered that I wouldn't take 'no' for an answer. I shared my belief that 'no' meant that he didn't KNOW enough about my great product offering to say 'YES'! He wasn't amused. He spent the next several minutes telling why he wanted to keep the current greeting card vendors he had and why he didn't want to deal with the headache of setting up and training a new vendor to service his Atlanta stores. I listened quietly and patiently as the AMD continued to explain his concerns about doing business with my company or any new vendor in his area. I gathered that this gentleman had worked his way up through the management ranks of Publix for the past 30+ years and was primarily responsible for the buying decisions of every Atlanta area store on behalf of his company. He was a Publix stockholder, therefore making him a part-owner in the company. His interest in the company's overall success was both professional and personal. I'm sure the AMD had to deal with a number of stressful vendor-related product and service issues on a regular basis. I'm also sure his massive responsibilities were probably a bit overwhelming at times. While praying for a positive turn in our conversation, God revealed to me that the ADM wasn't seeing me as a solution to *complement* sales and service; instead, he saw the addition of my product line as another potential vendor to *complicate* his life! Once given the opportunity to speak, I empathized with the many challenges the AMD faced on a daily basis. I assured him that I was determined to positively impact the success of his stores if given the opportunity to become a Publix vendor. The AMD eventually gave in and granted me a face-to-face meeting about a month out on his calendar.

While counting down to my meeting with the Publix AMD, God inspired me to reach out to the Publix Buyer again. This gentleman had been such a strong supporter of my company from the very beginning. I wanted to have further conversation with him on how to best prepare for my meeting with his peer, the AMD, and the best way to position myself for approval as one of their next greeting card suppliers. Perhaps the Publix Buyer could suggest other stores, outside of the Atlanta market, to carry my greeting card line. I needed a Plan B, just in case my meeting with the AMD was unsuccessful. I was determined to do business with Publix, no matter what it took. My Publix Buyer informed me that he would be transitioning his responsibilities to a new Greeting Card Buyer that had just been hired. He would be taking on the role of Buying Director. He suggested that I contact the new buyer to schedule an in-person meeting in the next week or so to get his opinion on my product line. As instructed, I contacted the new Publix Greeting Card Buyer immediately and scheduled a meeting him at his Lakeland, Florida office a few weeks out.

The day before my meeting with the new Publix Buyer, I took a flight from Atlanta to Orlando, Florida and rented a car. I stayed the night with my dear Aunt Frankie who lived in a beautiful lakefront community in the heart of Orlando. Early the next morning, I drove to Publix's Corporate Headquarters in Lakeland, Florida—about an hour from Orlando. I spent the majority of my trip along the Florida's Interstate 4—praising and talking to God. I had dreamed of an extremely successful meeting with the Publix Buyer the night before. I knew that God had already delivered the victory to me because I was on my way to meet with a buyer from *Publix Super Markets, Inc.!*

By the time I reached the security guard post for Publix's world headquarters, I was confident that God had already declared my victory as a Publix vendor. I was excited to give my name as an expected guest of the Publix Greeting Card Buyer. The security guard quickly confirmed my meeting via phone and directed me to park in a designated visitor's parking space near the front entrance of the large green glass building that housed their corporate offices.

Shortly after I checked in at the receptionist's desk, I was escorted back to the office of the Publix Buyer to begin my meeting. The new Greeting Card Buyer and I had positive chemistry from the beginning. He was rather young and energetic and was willing to listen to whatever I had to say. During our conversation, I discovered that I was the first vendor candidate the Greeting Card Buyer had scheduled to meet with in his newly appointed role. As the buyer looked through samples of my greeting card collection, he smiled at my artwork and commented quite favorably on the lighthearted messages and quality of my cards. As I progressed further along in my presentation, the former Greeting Card Buyer turned Buying Director stuck his head in the doorway to meet me in person. It was great to connect a face with the voice of the kind man who was primarily responsible for orchestrating my current meeting with the new Publix Greeting Card Buyer as well as my upcoming meeting with the Atlanta Merchandising Director. He even brought along his secretary to meet me—as she and I had shared several prior phone conversations together. The special attention the Publix leadership team showed me throughout my visit, made me feel like I was already a valued member of the Publix vendor family.

The Greeting Card Buyer asked a few more questions before informing me that he had decided to approve my company as a greeting card vendor for Publix Super Markets, Inc.! I was *ECSTATIC!* The buyer's verbal approval along with his promise to send a new vendor application package in the upcoming week was the beginning of a positive, prosperous relationship with one of the leading grocery store chains in the entire county! My PERSISTENCE had finally paid off! I thanked God, my *amazing CEO*, all the way back to the Orlando airport and throughout my flight back to Atlanta. I had traveled to Lakeland, FL expecting a victory with Publix and God, as He's done so many times in the past, *delivered!*

Once back in Atlanta, I began preparing for my meeting with the Publix AMD in the upcoming week. Since Publix corporate office was in the process of approving me as a vendor, I felt the deck was stacked in my favor for my meeting with the AMD. Ultimately, I wanted to be in the Atlanta stores more than anything. However, I was willing to go wherever I was sent for the honor serving one of the top companies in the country. Again, I prayed for a positive outcome to my upcoming meeting and left the end results in the very capable hands of my Heavenly CEO. When it comes to successful outcomes, God's winning record is unmatched!

The morning of my meeting with the AMD, I spent a few minutes praying to God for a favorable outcome including approval as a vendor for the Atlanta market and a fresh new start with the rather outspoken Publix leader. I pictured myself confidently articulating the merits of doing business with my company. As his secretary escorted me to the AMD's office, I said a quick prayer as I approached his open doorway. Upon entering his office, I found a rather distinguished-looking gentleman with neatly combed white hair—sitting behind a massive, immaculate mahogany desk. He stood up as I entered the room to greet me and shake my hand. He then invited me to have a seat on one of the two leather chairs positioned in front of his desk. I handed the AMD my business card and a meeting agenda of the topics I hoped to cover during our meeting. I also presented him with a folder which included a copy of my Company Overview, product brochure and service guarantee. I then asked him how much time I had to present the information. He gave me about thirty minutes to make my pitch.

The gentleman I met in person that day was nothing like the rather abrasive, angry gentleman I had spoken with on the phone a month or so earlier. Instead, the AMD was rather calm and extremely attentive. As I methodically moved through my Company Overview, I noticed the AMD chuckling at the messages of the sample greeting cards I had included in his folder. Once I completed my presentation, I answered any remaining service and distribution questions the AMD may have had. The AMD was adamant about my company being able to provide good customer service to any stores he would consider in his area. Great customer service was the trademark of Publix Super Markets, Inc. since the company's inception. He told me that SERVICE or the lack thereof would either make us extremely successful or eliminate our products from their stores rather quickly. With that understanding, the AMD was happy to inform me that he had reconsidered his decision and would be placing my greeting card collection in a select number of Publix stores in the Atlanta market! *I was ELATED!* I appealed to God for help to influence the AMD change his mind about giving my company a chance to service his Atlanta stores. Again, my God *delivered!*

Publix was just the business blessing we needed to begin building the #1 African-American female-owned greeting card company throughout the Southeast! Eventually our company was approved to go into almost **500** stores in Georgia, Florida, Tennessee, Alabama and South Carolina. An additional blessing, as a result of our approval as a Publix vendor, I followed back up with Kroger to determine if they would reconsider doing business with my company. The new Kroger buyer was so impressed by my unique greeting card collection; she immediately approved my company as a new vendor for over **200** Kroger Stores throughout the Southeast! Eventually that same Kroger buyer would play an instrumental role in my company receiving our first of many awards and honors in outstanding business accomplishments from the Atlanta business community. For several years, my company enjoyed our relationship as an approved vendor and supplier of quality greeting cards and gift items for the top two grocery giants in the country! Praise to God for the opportunity, perseverance and courage to pursue, win, learn and grow from our relationships with both Publix and Kroger!

The poem on the following page entitled, *Keep on Movin'*, has served as a great source of inspiration and motivation for me throughout career and in my quest to build a successful, world-class business enterprise. I hope it will inspire you to reach your career goals as well. Although the author is unknown, I thank him or her for providing the world with such encouraging words to inspire each of us to *keep moving* toward our goals and dreams everyday!

Keep on Movin'

When everything goes wrong
And you want to say 'so long'
. . . Keep on Movin'
When your friends aren't there
And no one seems to care
. . . Keep on Movin'

When everything's a fight
And nothing turns out right
. . . Keep on Movin'

When you don't get the promotion
And it feels like a demotion
. . . Keep on Movin'

When nobody's trained
And the team's lost its brain
. . . Keep on Movin'

When you don't hit your goal
And you're down in a hole
. . . Keep on Movin'

When there's someone to fire
Or someone to hire
. . . Keep on Movin'

When the customers are mad
Thinking you've done something bad
. . . Keep on Movin'

When sales are in the tank
Or there's no money in the bank
. . . **Keep on Movin'**

When customers are out the door
And you work 'til you're sore
. . . **Keep on Movin'**

When you feel betrayed
After all you've paid
. . . **Keep on Movin'**

When life is at its best
And you want to rest
. . . **Keep on Movin'**

When you've run the race
And you take first place
. . . **Keep on Movin'**

When you're on a winning streak
And the tea is at its peak
. . . **Keep on Movin'**

When your people shine
And everything's fine
. . . **Keep on Movin'**

When your goal is motivation
And you get great participation
. . . **Keep on Movin'**
When you get the raise
And enjoy the praise
. . . **Keep on Movin'**

When your goals are high
And you're shooting for the sky
. . . Keep on Movin'

When your sales are climbing
And the economy's rising
. . . Keep on Movin'

When you've faced a test
And you've done our best
. . . Keep on Movin'

When you've hit your goal
And you're on a roll
. . . Keep on Movin'

When everything is great
And it's time to celebrate
. . . Keep on Movin'

Summary:

When we decide to truly live without LIMITS, we can achieve amazing feats, we can go exciting places and we can reach bold new heights we only dreamed of before! My dear sweet Aunt Frankie used to tell me all the time, *'If it's to be, it's up to me!'* What she was telling me was "I" was the primary reason for any SUCCESS or FAILURES in life the decisions I made and the actions I took. Throughout my career, I achieved significant success when I decided to go where others were too lazy or too afraid to go. I have found that prayer, planning and patience DO pay off when GOD is consulted to open doors to lucrative business opportunities and promising promotions. The bigger we dream and back those dreams up with wisdom, work and worship to God on High—the greater our chances of achieving whatever conceivable goal we can imagine for our lives. What are you waiting on? Who are you waiting on to rescue you from your current dilemmas or career challenges? God is already standing by—ready to coach you to success. Seek His guidance to start believing, achieving and receiving the awesome life that He wants for you!

Exercise:

1. What three feats/goals would you accomplish if FEAR or FAILURE were not a concern?

2. *Envision the life you want for you and your family and then devise a plan to GO FOR IT!*

Affirmation:

"Lord, direct my feet on the path to SUCCESS by doing the things that will bring you praise and blessedness!"

Step #8

SURROUND Yourself with Positive People, Places and Things

"Finally, brothers, whatever is true, whatever is noble, whatever is right, whatever is pure, whatever is lovely, whatever is admirable—if anything is excellent or praiseworthy—think about such things."
Philippians 4:8 (NIV)

"Bloom Where You're Planted"

Have you ever had the privilege of being around people who make you feel good about yourself—just being in their presence? These people seem to always find just the right words to say to encourage you or to comfort you when you need it most? Perhaps these people were former CEOs or bosses at your present or former job. However, these people could also be family members, friends, co-workers, community leaders, business associates or acquaintances. Don't you wish there were more people like these precious gems in the world? Well, there can be!

You can make up your mind *today* to become a source of positive energy and inspiration for everyone around you. I'm not suggesting that you take some mood-altering drug or drink to send you into a state of superficial blissfulness or pretend to be someone you're not. I'm simply suggesting that by making a few positive changes in your life-style, your surroundings and the company of people you spend the majority of your time with, you can start to live your life in a more positive, productive, meaningful way each and every day.

I have always considered myself to be a positive, self-motivated *people person.* Although I can be pretty productive working alone, I thrive when I am in the presence of others—working as a team. During my 10+ years of working for a Fortune 100 company, my peers would often comment on how happy I appeared most of the time. Granted, I was still going through my fair share of trials and tribulations. I simply found it better to focus on the things I was grateful for, versus dwelling on my troubles. I chose not to let my momentary trials affect my attitude or negatively impact the people around me. I truly believe that God blesses us to be a blessing to others. I want everyone I encounter to feel God's presence in me through my smile, the way I dress, the way I walk and through the confident way I act and talk.

Another ritual I try to practice each day is to take the time to thank God for all my blessings—both great and small. This practice gives me plenty of reasons to be happy. I've learned not to worry about the things I don't have and the situations I can't change. Instead, I rely on God's grace and guidance to deliver me from evil and to arm me with the strength to overcome whatever challenges I will inevitably face throughout life. I have become more grateful for the blessings I used to take for granted such as good health, a loving, devoted family, a nice home in a safe neighborhood, reliable transportation, caring friends, our adorable, dog *Diamond*—just to name a few. I even thank God for the sunshine *and* the rain—for we need both to survive, thrive and sustain life!

At a past job as a Marketing Manager at a Fortune 500 corporation, I made my small cubicle office a "shrine of positivity". When co-workers entered my office—complaining about the work environment or the latest layoff rumor, I didn't want them to leave with the same negative outlook they entered with. So, I plastered my walls with powerful biblical scriptures, motivational poems, posters and quotes. I even wrote a 'positive quote for the day' on my dry erase every morning to share with co-workers who happened to glance at it as they walked past my office.

Once I left Corporate America to begin my own business, the first thing I created in my modest home-based office was a *positivity bulletin board.* I positioned it on the wall right next to my computer. The bulletin board is filled with positive memorabilia that bring me joy and positive reflection every time I look at it. It contains baby photos of my three sons, a picture of me as a size 6—with a lot of prayer and hard work—I plan to get back there one day! It also contains other inspirational messages and magnets to get me through tough challenges at work and at home. My positivity bulletin board is ever-changing. As exciting new events or experiences happen in my life, I update my positivity bulletin board to reflect my latest accomplishments or goals. It continues to inspire, motivate and encourage me to live my life with passion!

Summary:

Living positively or letting negativity consume your life is a choice. It's often as simple as choosing to surround yourself with positive, inspiring people, reading motivational books and poems, listening to uplifting audio recordings or electing to engage in activities that enhance your life and the lives of others. Regularly reading the Holy Bible can also provide you with an empowering foundation to overcome any storms or trials you may face. God has promised that He will protect us, keep us and love us *unconditionally* throughout the pages of His Word. Our faith increases when we spend more time reading His Word, praying for understanding of His Word and being a light in the world by actively practicing His Word.

Exercise:

1. *Make a list of the top three goals you would like to accomplish in the next year.*

2. *Create a 'Positivity' board by cutting out and pasting pictures or words on cardboard which describe your goals.*

3. *Post your Positivity board in a prominent location where you can see it often.*

4. *Take steps toward completing your goals each day until they are complete. Then, plan for your next three goals.*

Affirmation:

"I can do ALL things through Christ who strengthens me!"
Philippians 4:13

Step #9

DEDICATE Your Time and Talent to Serving Others

". . . Whoever wants to become great among you must be a servant, and whoever wants to be first must be your slave—just as the Son of man did not come to be served, but to serve, and to give His life as a ransom for man."
Matthew 20:26-28 (NIV)

"The Joy of Volunteering"

One of the most critically overlooked principles in the Bible is—we are not born into this world merely to serve our own selfish needs but to serve those of mankind as well. There is a special joy we can receive by dedicating our time and talents to helping others in need. *Volunteering* to help other less fortunate men, women, boys and girls in our society can give us a wonderful feeling of *fulfillment* and *purpose.*

We can start volunteering our time in a variety of different ways and for a number of different causes and reasons. Our volunteering efforts can start in our community via 'community clean-ups' or by starting a Neighborhood Watch program. In our church—we have the opportunity to volunteer for a variety of different ministries or to start a new ministry, depending upon the needs of our members and church community. We can participate in charity walks or runs sponsored through our employers or via community civic organizations. We can give financial donations to worthy causes such as United Way which supports a number of health-related initiatives. We can participate in the Empty Stocking Fund or a similar charitable cause which provides gifts for little girls and boys to open at Christmas. The United Negro College Fund allows us to contribute to the college educations of deserving young men and women of color. Or, we can find any number of nonprofit organizations in our communities to contribute our time, financial donations and talents to serving.

Over the past decade or so, one of the local non-profit organizations I've enjoyed supporting is the Atlanta Day Shelter for Homeless Women and Children. I began by adopting at least one shelter guest as a 'Secret Santa'. I picked up a list from the Shelter prior to Christmas which listed all the basic needs on one of their guests. Then, I went shopping for the items on the list, put them in a large gift bag and dropped it off at the shelter prior to Christmas Day with the individuals name and a copy of their wish list attached to it. Although I never got the opportunity to meet my Secret Santa recipient, my Christmas was blessed knowing that I had helped someone I didn't even know have a blessed, merrier Christmas.

The first time I visited the Atlanta Day Shelter, my heart grew heavy for the women and children I met there. The women were not much different from me or many of my friends. They were women from all walks of life and ethnicities. They were moms, daughters, aunts, grandmothers, wives and divorcees. These women had fallen on hard times and found themselves struggling to overcome the plight of 'homelessness' for a number of different reasons. As a mother of three young sons, I immediately made a connection with these women and the challenges they must be facing for the sake of their children. The responsibilities of motherhood are great enough. However, the uncertainty of where one's family will sleep each night, what they will eat and the challenges of keeping their kids safe from the treacherous city streets must be taxing daily decisions for many of the shelter's guests.

I recall meeting the founder and director of the shelter on one of my many visits to drop off clothing items. Ms. Ruth Schnatmeier, the Director of the Atlanta Day Shelter, was one of Gods angels here on earth. She provided leadership, comfort, protection and encouragement to the many broken souls she encountered on a daily basis. I spoke with Ruth about her shelter's needs and asked what we could do to help her achieve some of her objectives for the shelter. We discussed a few ideas. One of my friends, who was a local hair stylist, suggested that we do a 'Day of Beauty' to lift the spirits of the women at the shelter. I presented the idea to Ruth and she LOVED it! What better way to boost the self-esteem and inner-spirits of the women at the shelter than to beautify them from the outside—in. We planned our first 'Beautification Day' for the week before Mother's Day. I enlisted the support of my team of saleswomen from my greeting card company. My friend, the hair stylist, persuaded a number of her peers who were also hair stylists, barbers and nail technicians to volunteer their time and talents to this extremely worthy initiative. I secured donations from a number of restaurants and grocery stores for food items and beverages to support the event. We even received FREE hair care products from product distributors who were already doing business with a few of the hair stylists, God always makes a way for us to do his will. We took care of the needs of his homeless children and he took care of us.

While the mothers were being pampered, a few of our saleswomen who were also full-time teachers, entertained the children. The kids enjoyed participating in art contests, games and created colorful Mother's Day cards to surprise their moms. Everyone had a great time! Through the team effort of a few caring, self-less individuals, we brought a lot of smiles, joy and happiness to a number of broken, lost souls that afternoon.

The giving of your time, talents and financial gifts to an unselfish, worthy cause(s) can make a world of difference in the lives of others. The experience of volunteering can positively change your life too! I was inspired the write the following poem,

'The Volunteer', which expresses my true feelings about the JOY of volunteering. I hope it will inspire you to find a need in your community that you can dedicate your time, talents and resources to supporting.

The Volunteer

By Terri Rhem Robinson

The day I decided to **VOLUNTEER** was the day that changed my life.

The **V**alor of giving to a worthwhile cause was a feeling that was oh so nice.

I **O**ffered to give my time and talents to a cause that was worthwhile.

I **L**earned to share with others in need and to go that extra mile.

I **U**nderstood that volunteering was not a selfish act;

Instead I considered the **N**eeds of those whose futures I'd impact;

I learned that **T**eamwork was essential to work in harmony;

I **E**nlisted the gifts of myself and others to give most generously;

I **E**njoyed the journey along the way as we worked to support the cause;

And as we **R**eached our goals at last, I savored every applause!

Summary:

We each have unique talents, experiences and expertise we can use to inspire those around us to succeed! Our families, co-workers, business associates and communities should be blessed by the great works we do! Jesus Christ is the ultimate example of a man who came to earth, not to be served, but to serve and inspire others through His unselfish deeds and unparalleled, humanitarian acts of love. When faced with negativity or challenges in the workplace, at home or throughout life, ask yourself, *"What would Jesus do?"* Remember, only the things we do for God will last!

Exercise:

1. *Create a prayer list of family, friends and co-workers you will begin praying for on a regular basis?*

2. *What things can you do to serve the needy in your neighborhood?*

3. *What great cause can you adopt to contribute your time, talents and/or financial resources?*

4. *In the next week, identify at least 2 young people to share the importance of giving back and serving others.*

Affirmation:

"Lord, you are the Master of Giving. Help me to always appreciate and exercise the benefit of giving and to know that it is far more blest to give than it is to receive."

Step #10

INSPIRE Others to Follow God through Your Example

". . . Let your light shine before men, that they may see your good deeds and praise your father in heaven."
Matthew 5:16 (NIV)

"My Greatest Inspiration"

I began the introduction of this book by explaining how God inspired me to write, "Make God Your CEO". *Giving honor to God* is my ultimate purpose for printing personal testimonies about my career and the people who have impacted it throughout the pages of this book. I am happy to acknowledge His incredible influence in my life and to recap His wonderful blessings throughout my career. To God, I give all the credit and all the glory for whatever successes I have realized to date and in the future.

In addition, I have a few other important reasons for seeing this project through to completion. I have met so many people throughout my career who have needed encouragement, but didn't know how or where to go to find it. I have witnessed former peers ride the wave of career success and prosperity only to come crashing to the ground when their jobs or companies were suddenly eliminated, downsized or closed. Since I began writing this book over 15 years ago, I have personally experienced at least two jobs end *involuntarily* for me. The last one was almost a year ago when I was employed by a national non-profit organization as a Sponsorship Manager. While working remotely in my Atlanta home-based office, I received a phone call from my immediate supervisor on a Monday morning informing me that my position had been eliminated due to budgetary *constraints*. By the end of the call, my corporate email account and corporate cell phone had been de-activated and my family's health benefits would continue for just a few more short weeks. Like so many other *'suddenly unemployed'* individuals have experienced—there was little or no consideration for the impact on my family's personal well-being or financial security. Again, I called on God to sustain my family through this ordeal. Almost a year later, He continues to provide for us as I prepare to launch another exciting new career endeavor.

I wrote this book for former co-workers who moved themselves and/or their families across country for the sake of a new job opportunity only to have the opportunity taken away from them within a few short months after their relocations were complete. I also wrote this book for any individual who feels he or she is currently stuck in a dead-end, unrewarding job with little hope for promotion, satisfaction or change. This book is for those individuals who have allowed their internal fires to be doused by fear or accounts of their most recent failures. It is also for anyone who is procrastinating in using their God-given talents to pursue meaningful, fulfilling entrepreneurial ventures or to begin an exciting new project or endeavor. This book is for those individuals who continue to allow themselves to be victims of unfair workplace practices in exchange for a 'false sense of security'. If I haven't described your situation yet, not to fear, I wrote this book for *you* too!

I pray that by reading how I've been able to triumph over some of the challenges I've faced in my career, you will be blessed with courage, strength and determination to triumph over your trials as well. I don't profess to have the answer to every career or personal challenge you will face in life. I don't have all the answers, but *God does!* I pray that the powerful biblical scriptures, personal testimonies and motivational poems I've shared in this body of work will give you comfort, peace, hope and blessings in your time of need.

I don't believe that God wants us to limit our praise and relationship with Him to Wednesday night Bible Study, or during Saturday or Sunday church services. I do believe He wants us to call upon Him in the places where we spend the majority of our time outside of our homes and our places of worship. God seeks a relationship with us *on our jobs, in our businesses and throughout our careers!* ***God desires*** and ***deserves*** to be the ultimate CEO of our careers as well as our personal lives. We don't have to submit an e-mail request, employee application or bio to receive God's bountiful, blessings. God has a limitless amount of blessing inventory! There's no need to stand in long lines or spend hours in reception areas waiting on him to meet with us. We simply need to spend *quality time* with Him in daily prayer and by reading, obeying and sharing the principles of God's universal employee handbook—*the Holy Bible.*

Using our spiritual gifts to unselfishly serve others while consistently practicing God's biblical bylaws, will unlock the doors to unlimited opportunities, possibilities and success! I pray this book will arm you with the courage to take bold steps toward the career or business venture of your dreams. God has promised that He will fight *all* of our battles (both physical and spiritual) and make foot stools of our enemies! What better weapon than GOD to ensure our VICTORY in the trenches of unpredictable corporate warfare? Starting *today, right now, this very minute,* vow to make God *the* ultimate CEO of your life and prepare to open the door to a most meaningful, purpose-driven career blessed by the supernatural power of God's love, leadership and loyalty!

Summary:

God desires a close, intimate relationship with each of us in our personal and professional lives. The more we connect with Him through prayer and His Word, the more our life will mirror his image through our Lord and Savior Jesus Christ. There is no need to hang a banner outside of our cubicles or places of business—professing to be Christians. Others should see we are children of God through our speech, the way we dress, our overall demeanor and most importantly, through the way we treat others while conducting business. We should 'let our light shine' daily in our interactions with others so that they can SEE that God is the driving force that's guiding, protecting, maintaining, sustaining and prospering us.

Exercise:

1. *What one thing can you begin TODAY to bring more glory and honor to God?*

2. *What negative habit(s) are you committed to giving up in order to draw closer to God (Smoking? Drinking? Over-eating? Promiscuity?)*

3. *Make a list of up to six things you can do to positively enhance your relationship with God. (Example: Pray and read the Holy Bible each day; Volunteer to help the needy; Join and/or attend a local church regularly; Actively volunteer in a church ministry)*

Affirmation:

"I am highly blessed! I'm highly favored! My future is bright! My career is promising! And, God is CEO of my life!"

About the Author

Terri Rhem Robinson is an award-winning businesswoman, nationally renowned motivational speaker, marketing consultant and parenting coach. Formerly recognized as the Atlanta Business League's "Outstanding Home-based Business" winner, Robinson enjoys sharing her Christian-based business practices to aspiring entrepreneurs and employees everywhere! As an inspiring Parenting Coach, Robinson shares her positive football-based practices for building stronger, happier 'home teams' with families, schools and non-profits throughout the country. She resides in Mableton, Georgia (an Atlanta suburb) with her husband, Rodric, of 25+ years and their three young sons, Carl, Jordan and Christopher.

Terri has been featured in a number of local, regional and national business and trade publications. She has also been featured on several radio and television talk shows—sharing her philosophies on success in faith, family, business and life. For more information on Terri Robinson, to order more copies of her book or to book her to speak at an upcoming event, please email her at connect2coacht@gmail.com.

***Make God Your CEO** delivers a proven game plan—to help you recharge your career, boost the success of your business and walk in VICTORY everyday! Discover 10 spiritual steps that will lead you move up a promising career path to unlock the door to God's bountiful blessings. This book will prepare you to FOCUS on what you really want in life while inspiring you to TRUST in GOD to help you achieve your dreams!*